Lucinda Mackworth-Young

Piano by ear

Learn to play by ear, improvise
and accompany songs
in simple steps

FABER *ff* MUSIC

Acknowledgements

There are many people who have helped inspire and develop this book: my own teachers who gave me a sound, conventional music education, and my sisters with whom I first experienced the joy and freedom of spontaneous improvisation (with *Chopsticks* and *Heart and soul*, as children do!). Lettice Stuart at Trinity College of Music who taught we undergraduates that pupils learn through making their own music, and Director of Music, Richard Townend, at Hill House School, who entrusted me with piano classes in which I first taught group improvising. Also the ISM and EPTA, who enabled me to continue developing ideas through giving workshops.

Fellow professors at The Piano Teachers' Course EPTA UK, especially Sally Cathcart who suggested *Sing then Play* and supported the introduction of playing by ear and improvising workshops on the course, and the PTC students who so enthusiastically used the material with their own pupils.

It is impossible to mention everyone, but the following teachers and students have been especially helpful in trialling material and suggesting ideas: Alanna Frieda, Anne-Laure Condat, Chris Middleton, David Moss, Diane Gelon, Fiona Harman, Fiona Page, George Every, Gila Robinson, Helena Newsom, Hugo Sells, Jane Lakey, Jennifer Poole, Jenny Sharples, Jo Weller, Julia Tash, Julie Reeman, Julie Cooper, Kate Moore, Kath Hutchinson, Liz Giannopoulos, Megan Beynon, Michael Bull, Monica Ali, Oma Emosivwe, Samantha Kember, Shaun Adams, Sonum Batra, Sue Martin and Wendy Jackson. Also Rosie Sells, who helped with her at-a-glance appraisal, and Kathryn Clyde who proofread.

Colleagues Nigel Scaife (ABRSM) and Chris Walters (Trinity) warmly affirmed the need for such a book, similarly Paul Harris, who suggested that I contact Lesley Rutherford directly.

My husband, Oliver Sells, also deserves a mention for his support (and toleration of many a disturbed early morning and kitchen table piled high with manuscript!).

Finally it is owing to the huge interest and expertise of Lesley, Lucy Holliday and everyone at Faber Music that the book has been pulled into proper shape and reached publication.

A big thank you to you all!

© 2015 by Faber Music Ltd
This edition first published in 2015
Bloomsbury House 74–77 Great Russell Street London WC1B 3DA
Text designed by Susan Clarke
Cover design by Chloë Alexander
Printed in England by Caligraving Ltd

ISBN10: 0-571-53902-5
EAN13: 978-0-571-53902-4

To buy Faber Music publications or to find out about the full range of titles available please contact your local music retailer or Faber Music sales enquiries:
Faber Music Ltd, Burnt Mill, Elizabeth Way, Harlow CM20 2HX
Tel: +44 (0) 1279 82 89 82 Fax: +44 (0) 1279 82 89 83
sales@fabermusic.com fabermusicstore.com

Contents

Introduction

This book is for everyone who wants to be able to play _without music books_. It's for those who've played the piano for many years in the traditional way, reading notes, and who long to be able to play by ear and improvise. It's also for those who are less experienced, but have some note-reading ability, and for beginners working with a teacher.* There's something for everyone.

- **Think of the ideas as starting points.** Follow them to the letter (they do work!) or adapt them to suit you.

- **Keep it light, easy and fun.** Do not attempt exercises that are too difficult to be enjoyable.

- **If you are working with a teacher**, he or she can play the right-hand tune while you work out the left-hand chords, and vice versa. You can also have fun improvising together.

- **Play the right- and left-hand notes given at the top of each page.** They are the notes, chords and fingering needed for that page.

- **Practise hands separately as well as together.** The more each hand knows what it's doing the easier it is to put both hands together.

- **Use consistent fingering**: finger memory plays an important part in helping you find the right notes and chords.

- **Constantly review.** Playing by ear and improvising are skills that develop and deepen when reviewing _known_ material as well as when you learn something new. The more familiar it becomes the easier you will find it to improvise, and the more fun you will have.

- **Reviewing also helps you _remember_ what you can play** for those spontaneous moments when you spot a piano somewhere, and don't have your books!

Feel free to try, make mistakes, and try again. Be pleased with every bit of progress. And from time to time stop to look at the view: remind yourself what you _can_ do and _have_ achieved. If you are new to the piano, your main challenge may be getting the right finger to work at the right time. If you've played for many years reading notes, you may feel frustrated that your eyes remain quicker and more accurate than your ears! Be patient with your developing skills, whatever they are, and aim to make your journey enjoyable. And above all, be guided by your own musical instinct and have fun!

Lucinda

*See also _Notes and accompaniments for teachers_ on page 122.

Visit _www.lucinda-mackworth-young.co.uk/piano-by-ear_ for further help and information.

Playing a tune by ear

Beginning with black notes

There are fewer black notes than white, which helps when beginning to play by ear. They form a variety of five-note (**pentatonic**) scales which sound wonderful to improvise with.

Using lyrics

When playing by ear, you need to be able to hear the music *inside your head*. Lyrics can help you remember tunes you already know, and they provide a structure to help you work out the musical building blocks needed. These musical building blocks are:

- **Pulse:** the regular, underlying beat
- **Rhythm:** the length of notes and how they are grouped together in patterns over time
- **Pitch:** the rise and fall of notes in relation to each other
- **Key or tonality:** the group of notes needed (the **scale**), and their 'home' base
- **Melody:** the tune
- **Harmony:** chords and their progressions
- **Form:** the overall architecture.

What if I can't hear the music well enough in my head?

Don't worry! You can find well-known songs online. Listen as often as you need to.

How to begin

- Choose the tune you know best from the two below.
- Find the hand position and notes indicated on the keyboard (black notes only).
- Play the starting note (given as a finger number under the title) and sing the tune. As you sing, notice:
  - The regular, underlying **pulse** – tap your foot to help you.
  - The rise and fall of **pitch**.
  - The number of **phrases** (there are usually four) and whether any repeat.
- Now play the tune, guided by your ear. Write in any fingering to help you.
- Practise until you can it play confidently and musically, without looking at the book.

Right-hand position
(four notes)

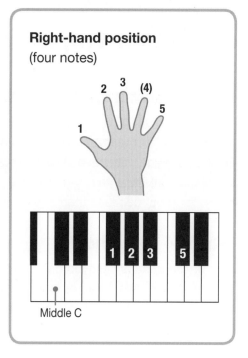

Middle C

Merrily we roll along

(finger 3)

3   2   1   2 etc — Fingering
Merrily we roll along,

Roll along, roll along,

Merrily we roll along,

All the live-long day.

Similar song

Going home (finger 3) from Dvořák's
New World Symphony

Mary had a little lamb

(finger 3)

Mary had a little lamb,

Little lamb, little lamb,

Mary had a little lamb,

Its fleece was white as snow.

Tip

Humming helps: if you're not sure whether the next note is higher or lower than the last, hum the song and notice the feeling inside you: it rises and falls in line with the pitch.

7

Accompanying a tune by ear

How do I accompany a tune by ear?

The simplest way to accompany tunes is to play **open 5th chords** on the **key-note** (or 'home note'). This is the note that makes the music sound finished. As you may have already discovered when playing these tunes on the black notes, the key-note is F♯, so the open 5th chord is F♯ and C♯. The chord is 'open' because there are no notes in between F♯ and C♯.

When do I play chords?

Chords are generally played on the **strong beats**. Strong beats occur regularly, every two, three or four beats, depending on the song. **Typically there are eight strong beats per song.** Longer songs tend to have twelve, sixteen or more, in multiples of four.

Does every phrase begin with a strong beat and chord?

No, sometimes there will be **upbeats** at the beginning of phrases. An upbeat is played (rhythmically) just before the strong beat on which the chord is played. Strong beats are also known as **downbeats** and they are the first beat of the bar in written music.

How to begin

- Sing or say the words of the tune you've worked out by ear in strict rhythm to feel the pulse and the regular **strong beats**. (Tap your foot to help.)
- Underline the syllables which fall on the strong beats.
- Find the left-hand open 5th chord on the keyboard (black notes only).
- Sing the tune while you play this chord on each underlined syllable. Make sure any **upbeats** are fitted in before the **downbeats**, without taking extra time.
- Practise hands together until you can play it confidently and musically, without looking at the book.

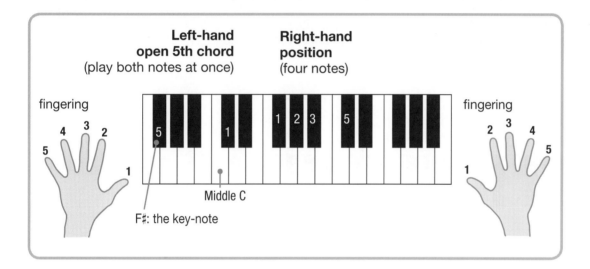

Left-hand open 5th chord (play both notes at once)

Right-hand position (four notes)

fingering

Middle C

F♯: the key-note

fingering

Merrily we roll along

(finger 3)

3 2 1 2 etc ——— Fingering

<u>Merri</u>ly we <u>roll</u> along,

Roll along, roll along,

Merrily we roll along,

All the live-long day.

Mary had a little lamb

(finger 3)

Mary had a little lamb,

Little lamb, little lamb,

Mary had a little lamb,

Its <u>fleece</u> was white as snow.

Upbeat   Downbeat

Similar song

Going home (finger 3) from Dvořák's New World Symphony

Tip

Feel the beat and play as rhythmically as possible.

Three-note tunes

Play the tune by ear:

- Play the starting note (given by the title) and sing the tune to make sure you know it.
- Play it by ear (black notes only). Write in any fingering to help you.

Then accompany it:

- Sing or say the words in strict rhythm to find the strong beats where chords will be played.
- Underline the syllables which fall on those strong beats.
- Sing the tune while you play the left-hand open 5th chord on the strong beats.
- Practise hands together until you can play it without looking at the book.

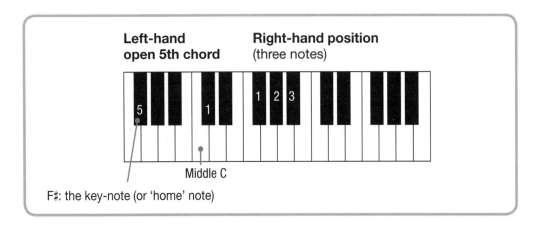

Left-hand open 5th chord

Right-hand position (three notes)

Middle C

F♯: the key-note (or 'home' note)

Au clair de la lune (thumb)

1 1 1 2 etc ────── Fingering
<u>Au</u> clair de la <u>lune</u>,

Mon ami Pierrot,

Prête-moi ta plume

Pour écrire un mot.

Tip

Try each note systematically until you find the right one.

Bad Moon Rising (finger 3)

I see the bad moon arising. __

I see trouble on the way. __

I see earthquakes and lightnin'. __

I see bad times today. __

These are 'silent' downbeats: no words are sung, but a left-hand chord is needed.

Similar songs to try

Fais dodo (finger 3)
Hot cross buns (three-note version) (finger 3)
Suogan (thumb)

Five-note tunes

Let's try some tunes with more notes. Follow the same steps as for
the three-note tunes:

- Play the starting note (given by the title) and sing the tune.
- Play it by ear (black notes only). Write in any fingering to help you.
- Sing or say the words in strict rhythm to find the strong beats.
- Underline the syllables which fall on those strong beats.
- Sing the tune while you play the left-hand open 5th chords.
- Practise hands together, without looking at the book.

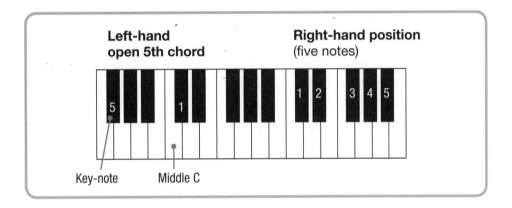

Left-hand open 5th chord

Right-hand position (five notes)

Key-note   Middle C

Tom Dooley (thumb)

1   1   2   3 etc.
<u>Hang</u> down your head, Tom <u>Dooley</u>,

Hang down your head and cry,

Hang down your head, Tom Dooley,

Poor boy, you're bound to die.

Old Macdonald (finger 3)

3   3   3   1   etc.
<u>Old</u> Macdonald <u>had</u> a farm,

Ee i ee i oh!

| Upbeat |
And <u>on</u> that farm he had some chicks,

| Downbeat | Ee i ee i oh!

 Tip

Head for the downbeats, slipping in any upbeats just before.

Similar song

- *Mull Of Kintyre* Wings (thumb)

Beginning to improvise

Improvising is simple. It's just playing notes that are inspired by something: often a song or piece, but it can be anything – a thought, feeling, thing of beauty, picture or story. Notes and accompaniments are chosen to suit the feeling of the music (and ability of the player), and the whole thing is held together by a structure that relies on a consistent pulse.

How do I begin?

The simplest way is to use the rhythm of a song or rhyme that you know well. The rhythm provides a ready-made structure that's just waiting for you to place your own notes on it.

Which notes do I play?

You will be given particular hand positions, scales and chords that sound good. To start with we'll use the five-note (pentatonic) scale that you've been using to play by ear. This works well when improvising because nothing sounds wrong when played together: everything 'works'!

How do I play them?

The point is to play beautifully, simply and naturally. Try to move mostly by step (up and down or down and up). Of course, you can play the notes in any order you like, especially when you have more experience and confidence in your inner ear. But until then, just let the notes flow up and down and don't try too hard. Music comes from intuitive feeling, rather than clever thinking.

What if it sounds wrong?

So long as you maintain a secure pulse and can direct your fingers to play rhythmically, the given notes are unlikely to sound wrong. They may sound *unexpected*, as it takes a while for your inner hearing to connect fully with the notes your fingers are playing. If you do find yourself playing any unexpected notes, just keep going, as though you intended them all along.

How do I make it mean something?

Again, a secure pulse is the key. If your left hand is consistent and rhythmical and you play beautifully, the music will make perfect sense and will transport you and your listeners. Think about colouring your music to match your feelings and imagination (warmth and sunshine, perhaps) and imagine themes or titles to inspire you ('A beach at sunset' or 'A night on the town').

How to begin

- *Say* (don't sing) the words of *Old Macdonald* in strict rhythm.
- Then *play* the right-hand notes up and down in the rhythm as you *say* all the words, and you will have improvised four phrases! Play black notes only (every note has a sharp).

Try it hands together:

- Set a steady pulse and improvise with the right-hand notes (in the rhythm of *Old Macdonald*) over the left-hand open 5th chord.
- The opening phrase is suggested: continue simply and naturally.
- Bring your improvisation to a musically satisfying end (usually on the key-note).
- Practise until you can play fluently and musically without looking at the book.

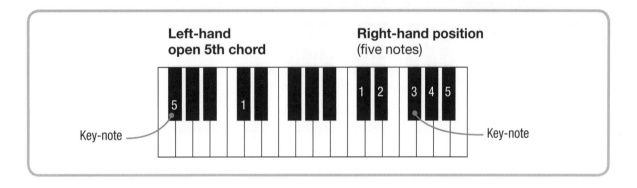

Improvise in the rhythm of *Old MacDonald*

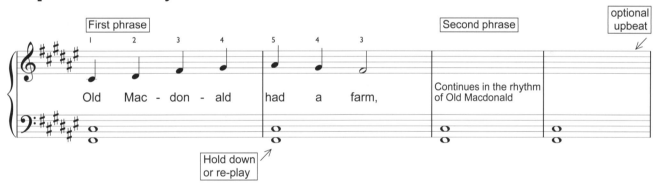

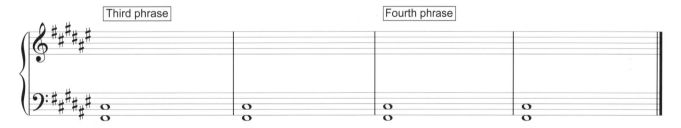

Give your improvisation meaning

Remember to play beautifully and use your imagination to 'colour' the sound. You could imagine Old Macdonald working on his farm and be inspired to play energetically, happily and moderately loudly. Or you could be thinking of a Scottish mountain scene and play gently. Giving your improvisation a title can help.

Tip

Always feel the beat and keep going even if a note sounds unexpected. No one knows what was intended, except you!

More improvising

This time we'll use two left-hand chords.

- Set a steady pulse and play the four-bar left-hand as an introduction.
- Improvise four right-hand phrases (two bars each) over the chords. Notice the suggested opening phrase descends then ascends and starts with the fifth finger. You can continue using the rhythm of *Old MacDonald* if you like.
- Play black notes only (every note has a sharp).
- Remember to bring your improvisation to a musically satisfying end.

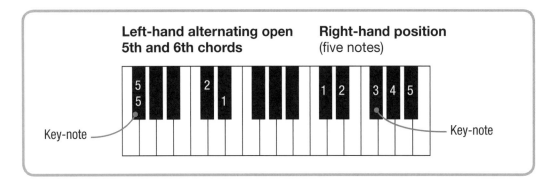

A sunny day

Try another improvisation using the rhythm of a different song, perhaps *Mary had a little lamb*, *Mull of Kintyre* or *Jack and Jill* (it has a great swing rhythm). *Hedwig's Theme* (John Williams) also works well, but does begin on an upbeat.

Tip *If you don't like the note you're on, move to the one next door!*

Solo and group improvising on black notes

To play solo:

- Choose one **left-hand repeated bass** and one **right-hand position** and improvise in the usual way.
- Remember to set a steady pulse and play four left-hand bars as an introduction.
- Bring your improvisation to an end on the key-note and chord (F♯).

To play with two or more people:

- The leader must play a **left-hand repeated bass.**
- Everyone else chooses either left or right hand or hands together.
- The leader sets a steady pulse and guides left-hand players to enter at two-bar intervals. Then right hands players enter, listening and responding to each other.
- Players can bring their own parts to an end individually, or be guided to a close on the key-note and chord (F♯).

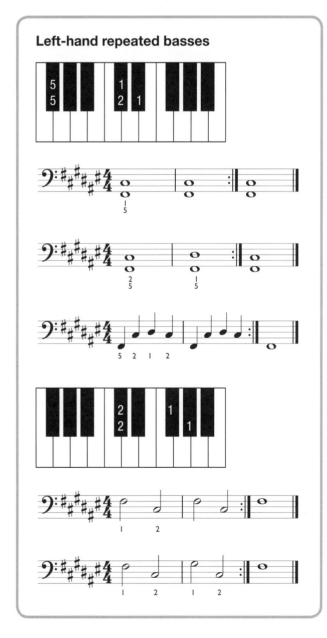

Left-hand repeated basses

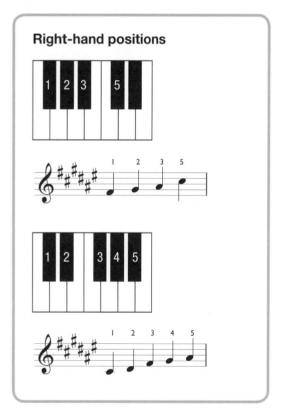

Right-hand positions

Tip

Anyone (even non-pianists) can join in because all black notes can be played at once without sounding wrong. Just maintain a steady pulse and a rhythmic left hand throughout.

Chords

Chords are built in **triads**. A triad consists of the first (also known as the **root**), third and fifth notes of a scale. Chords are named by the root note; this commonly appears above the stave in music. They can also be named by a **Roman numeral** (chord I), which indicates their position within the key. Another name for chord I in any key is the **tonic** chord. Playing each note of the triad in turn (starting at the bottom) is called a **broken chord**.

Chord I in C major

Practise the C chord blocked and broken, as shown, with the fingering given.

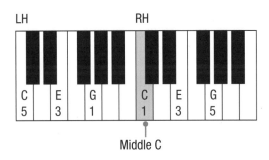

Middle C

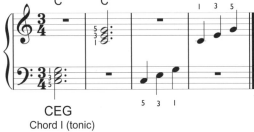

CEG
Chord I (tonic)

The grand arpeggio in C major

- Begin on the lowest C on the piano and play six broken chords with alternate hands, crossing left hand over right hand to continue up the keyboard.
- Finish with your left-hand index finger crossing over your right hand to play a top C.
- Hold the pedal down throughout and listen to the wonderful effect!
- Use consistent fingering so you can feel, learn and remember the hand shape.

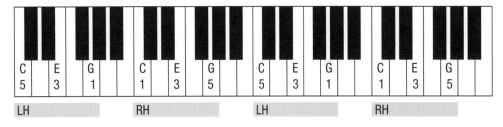

Continue up the keyboard …

Chord V in C major

Chord V is a triad built on the fifth note of the scale, which is also called the **dominant**. In C major the fifth note is G, and the root, third and fifth notes of the G chord are G, B and D:

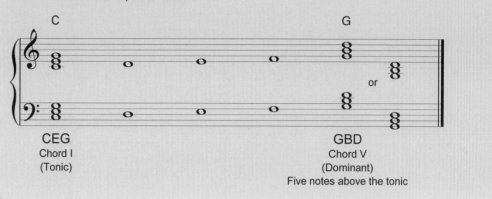

CEG
Chord I
(Tonic)

GBD
Chord V
(Dominant)
Five notes above the tonic

The G grand arpeggio

- Play the G grand arpeggio from the bottom to the top of the piano, as shown.
- Hold the pedal down throughout.

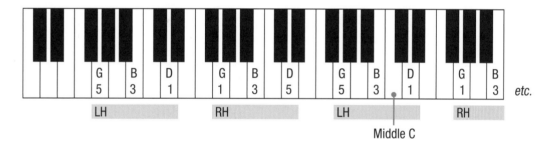

Middle C

A grand arpeggio progression

- Now play the C grand arpeggio, carry straight on with the G grand arpeggio and finish with the C grand arpeggio again.
- You will need to change the pedal for each grand arpeggio.
- Notice that the C grand arpeggio is needed after the G grand arpeggio to bring the music back 'home' and make it sound finished.

Inversions of chords

In order to move comfortably and musically from one chord to another, **inversions** are often used. The chord contains the same notes, but the position of the notes change.

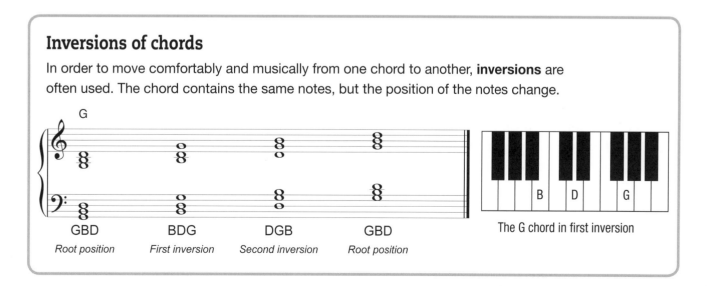

GBD
Root position

BDG
First inversion

DGB
Second inversion

GBD
Root position

The G chord in first inversion

Home and away chords

Practise this five-finger position and chord progression, hands separately and together, with the correct fingering, until completely secure and comfortable:

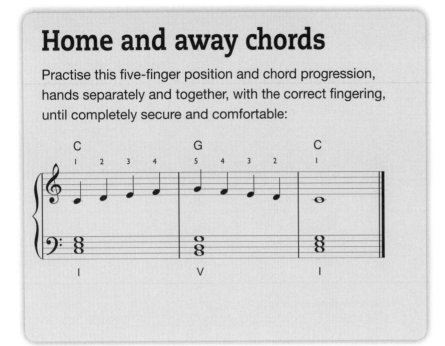

Right-hand C five-finger position

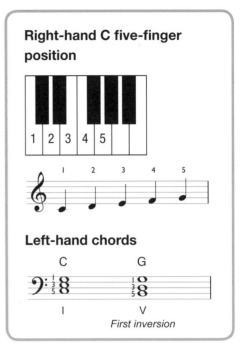

Left-hand chords

Harmonise the melody below with one left-hand chord per right-hand note. Write your chosen chord using a symbol (C or G) in each box. Notice the 'extra' chord needed in the penultimate bar to bring the music back 'home'.

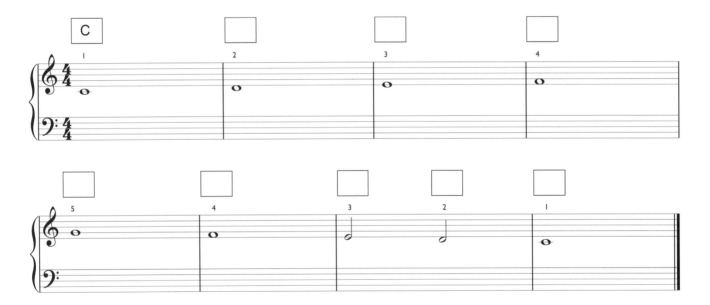

Key chords

The C chord is the **key** (or 'home') **chord** in C major. A chord of G can be thought of as the 'away' chord in this key. It creates a contrasting tension which needs to be resolved (or brought back home) to C.

Tip

The chord which sounds best usually includes the melody note. Follow the given fingering.

Accompanying with two chords

Play the tune by ear

- You have already played this tune on the black notes: now try it in the key of C major.
- Write in any notes and fingering to help you.

Accompany it with two chords

- Sing or hum the tune while you try out the chords, one on each strong beat.
- Write your chosen chord symbol in each box.
- Practise it until you can play hands together without looking at the book!

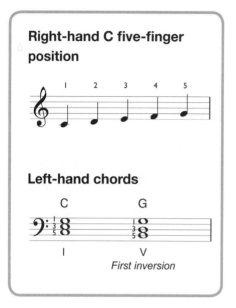

Right-hand C five-finger position

Left-hand chords

First inversion

Merrily we roll along

Chord symbol

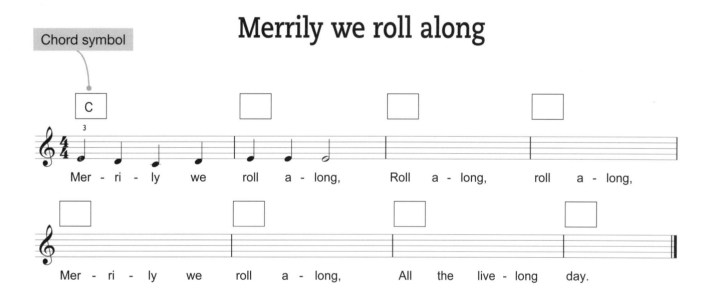

Mer - ri - ly   we   roll   a - long,   Roll   a - long,   roll   a - long,

Mer - ri - ly   we   roll   a - long,   All   the   live - long   day.

Lead sheets

If you chose to fill in all the melody notes and chord symbols you would have created a **lead sheet**. This is a form of music notation which gives the three essential elements of a song: the melody in conventional notation, the lyrics written below the stave, and the chords written in symbols above the stave.

Tip

Stick to the chord you're on until you can hear the need to change it.

Similar songs to try

- *Aunt Nancy* (*Aunt Rhody*) (begins on E)
- *Mary had a little lamb* (begins on E)
- *Pease pudding hot* (begins on C)

Accompanying singing

When people are singing or playing the tune on another instrument, you don't need to play the tune on the piano. You can just play the chords, with both hands, to provide a simple and supportive accompaniment. It sounds good, is easy to do and very useful.

- The root of the chord is usually played by the left hand with full chords in the right, but you can play full chords in both hands.

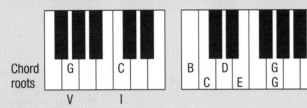

- Notice that the root of Chord V (G) is four notes *below* as well as five notes *above* the root of Chord I (C). It sounds stronger to play the G *below*.
- These chords are all in root position despite the right-hand notes, because the lowest (left-hand) note is the **root**.

Let's get playing

The songs below can all be accompanied by this chord progression:

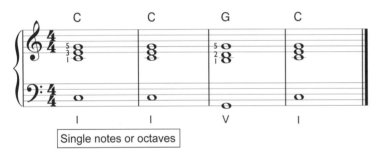

- Practise the progression above as shown.
- Choose a song, play the starting note and sing or hum the tune while you play the progression.
- Then try playing the chords in the catchy 4-time rhythm given below (the words to *London Bridge* are given as an example).

> **Tip**
>
> *Songs with the same chord progression can be sung simultaneously!*

Merrily we roll along (begins on E)

Mary had a little lamb (begins on E)

Aunt Nancy (begins on E)

Pease pudding hot (begins on C)

London Bridge (begins on G)

Pizza hut (begins on C)

The lonely goatherd from *The sound of music* (begins on G below middle C)

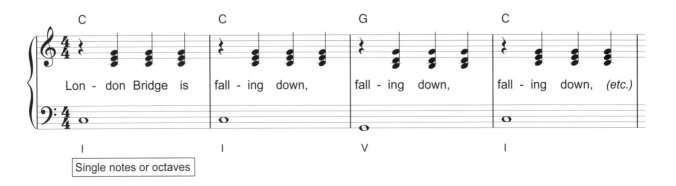

Adding sevenths to chords

The seventh note above the root is sometimes added to give chords extra tension. It is most common to add a seventh to chord V (the dominant). This is then called the **dominant seventh** or, in Roman numerals, **V⁷**.

The dominant seventh in C major: G⁷

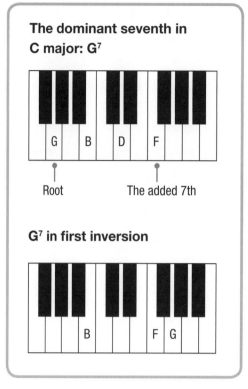

Dominant sevenths inverted

Dominant sevenths are often inverted, with the fifth note (D in this case) omitted to make it more comfortable to play.

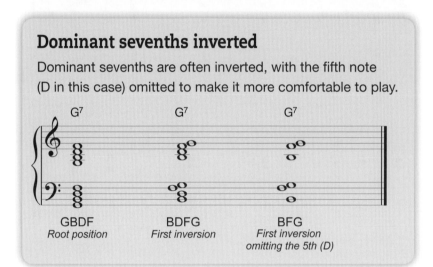

Home and away chords with an added seventh

Practise these two C, G⁷, C (home and away) progressions hands separately and together with the correct fingering until completely secure and comfortable.

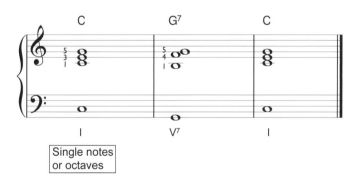

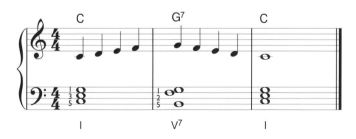

21

The 'Chopsticks' chord progression

Can you play *Chopsticks*? If so, play it in the usual way on black notes, and listen to the chord progression.

Here is *Chopsticks* in C major. Notice the chord progression:

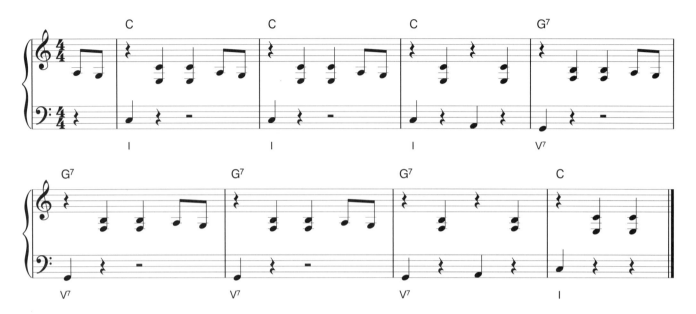

Chord progressions written down

Chord progressions are often written using symbols and slashes. Each symbol or slash represents one beat, so the '**Chopsticks**' chord progression in C major would be written like this:

Or, using Roman numerals:

C / / / C / / / C / / / G⁷ / / /　　**I / / / I / / / I / / / V⁷ / / /**

G⁷/ / / G⁷/ / / G⁷/ / C / / /　　**V⁷/ / / V⁷/ / / V⁷/ / / I / / /**

The following songs can all be accompanied by this chord progression, and can be sung simultaneously.

- Practise the progression in the rhythmic accompaniment style below.
- Then choose a song, play the starting note and sing or hum the tune while you play the progession. (The words to *My old man* are given as an example.)

One man went to mow (begins on E)
My old man's a dustman (begins on E)
Polly wolly doodle (begins on C, and has an upbeat)

> **Tip**
>
> *When the singing is well underway, play Chopsticks in C major as the accompaniment!*

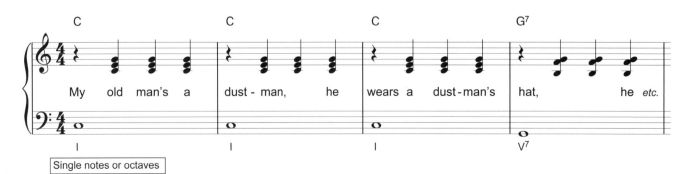

Single notes or octaves

'Home' and 'away' cadences

A **cadence** is the two-chord progression found at the ends of phrases, sections and pieces of music. The two most common cadences are the **perfect cadence**: chord V then chord I, and the **imperfect cadence**: chord I (or any chord) then chord V. The perfect cadence brings the music back 'home', making it sound finished. The imperfect cadence takes the music 'away', leaving it sounding unfinished.

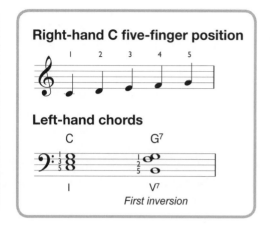

Practise these cadences, hands separately and together, with the correct fingering, until completely secure and comfortable.

Perfect cadences (coming home)

Imperfect cadences (going away)

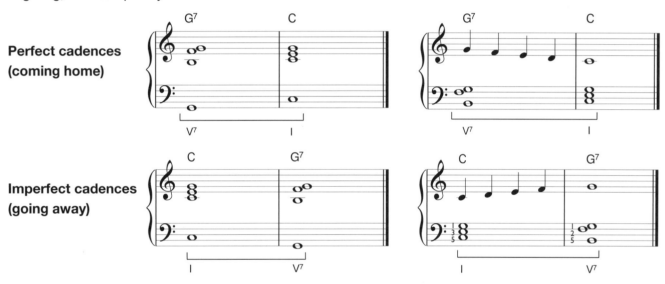

- Work out the tune of *One man went to mow*, writing in any notes or fingering.
- Sing the tune while you try out the chords, one on each strong beat.
- Write your chosen chord symbol in each box. Notice the two cadences.
- Practise hands together until you don't need the book.

One man went to mow

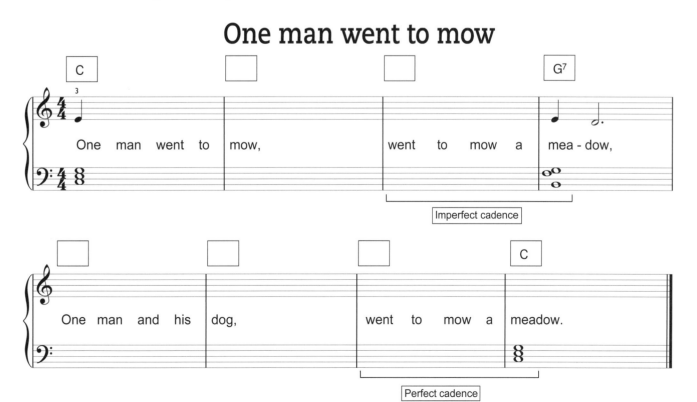

One man went to mow, went to mow a mea - dow,

One man and his dog, went to mow a meadow.

23

Melody and harmony

Melodies include **harmony notes** (notes in the chord), **passing notes** (notes which pass between chord notes) and **clashing notes**. The clashing notes tend to resolve onto harmony notes on the following beat.

- Play the tune by ear, writing in any notes and fingering to help you.
- Sing or hum the tune while you try out the chords and write your chosen chord symbol in each box. Notice that many of the bars need two chords in the second half. It adds a feeling of intensity to the music.
- Practise it hands together until you don't need the book.

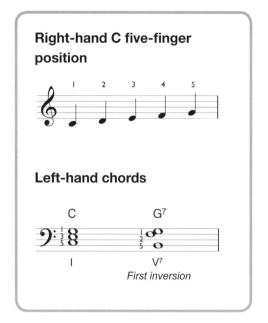

Right-hand C five-finger position

Left-hand chords

Ode to joy

Ludwig van Beethoven

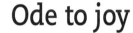

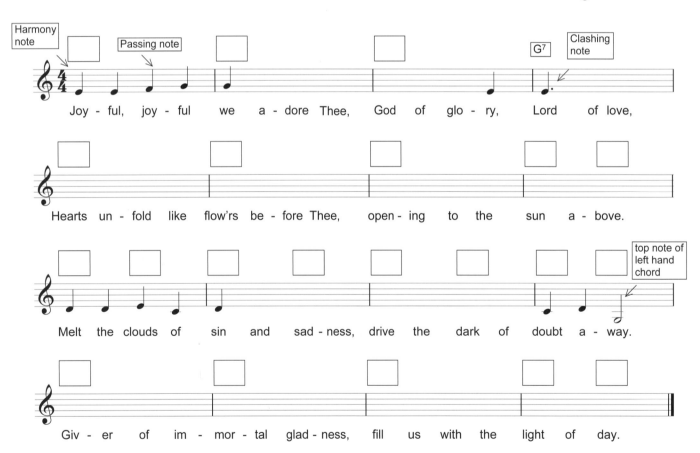

Similar songs and tunes to try

Going home (begins on E) from Dvořák's *New World Symphony*
Lightly row (begins on G)

Chord IV in C major

Chord IV is built on the fourth note of the scale, which is also called the **subdominant**. In C major the fourth note is F, and the root, third and fifth notes of the F chord are F, A, C. Here it is with the other chords you've learnt so far in C major:

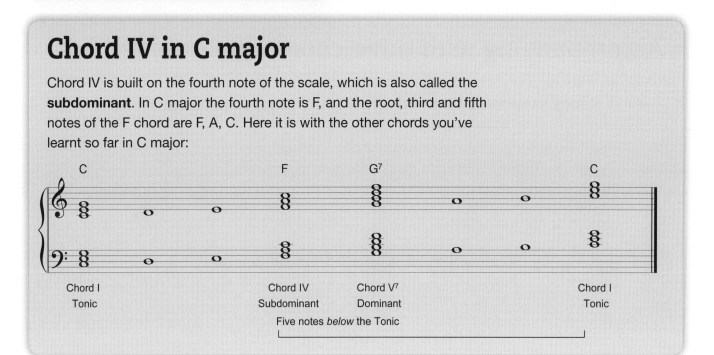

Chord I		Chord IV	Chord V⁷			Chord I
Tonic		Subdominant	Dominant			Tonic

Five notes *below* the Tonic

The F grand arpeggio

- Play the F grand arpeggio from the bottom to the top of the piano, as shown.
- Remember to use the pedal.

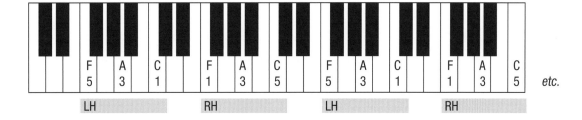

The F chord inverted

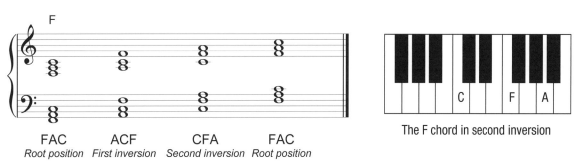

FAC	ACF	CFA	FAC
Root position	*First inversion*	*Second inversion*	*Root position*

The F chord in second inversion

Play these broken chords in the positions and inversions shown, firmly and warmly with the correct fingering, to help your fingers feel and remember them:

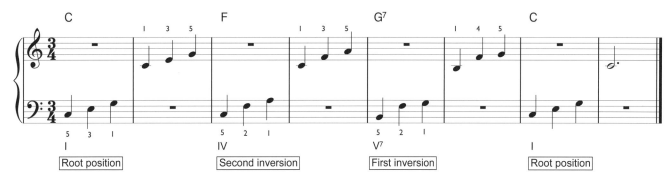

25

Accompanying with three chords in C major

- Practise this scale and chord progression, hands separately and together until completely secure and comfortable.
- Make sure you use the fingering given.

You will find this chord progression very useful for playing by ear, improvising and transposing. Notice that the scale, played as a melody, includes harmony notes, passing notes and clashing notes.

Primary chords

Chords I, IV and V (and V⁷) are known as the **primary chords** in any key. They include all of the notes of the scale between them, so they are often the only chords needed when accompanying a tune.

This melody can be accompanied by all three primary chords in C major:

- Play the tune on its own first.
- Then play the tune while you work out the chord for each bar and write in the chord symbols.
- Play the piece hands together.

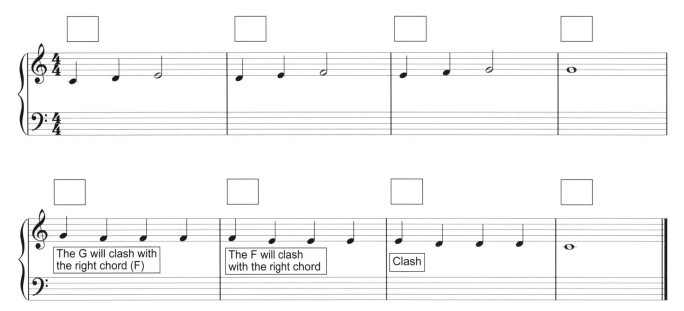

The G will clash with the right chord (F)

The F will clash with the right chord

Clash

Writing out chord progressions

- Work out the tune by ear, writing in any fingering.
- Say the words in strict rhythm to find and underline the strong beats.
- Sing or hum the tune while you work out the chords and write in chord symbols beneath the lyrics.
- Write the chord progression in the boxes given. (This is an easy way to see and remember it.)
- Practise it hands together, listening rather than looking at the book.

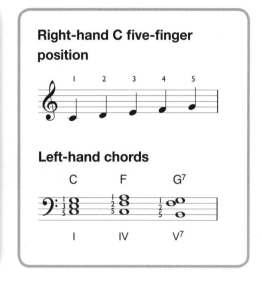

Right-hand C five-finger position

Left-hand chords

When the saints (begins on C)

Fingering

Upbeats Oh when the saints go marching in, Oh when the saints go marching in,

Chord symbol

Oh how I want to be in that number, When the saints go marching in.   Clash

Extra chord

Write in the chord progression:

C / / / ☐ / / / ☐ / / / ☐ / / /

☐ / / / ☐ / / / ☐ / ☐ / ☐ / /

Similar songs

Beautiful brown eyes The Brothers Four (begins on E)
Bye bye love Everly Brothers (begins on F with the F chord)
Our house Madness (begins on C)
One more night Phil Collins (begins on E)

Tip

Swing low *can be sung at the same time as* When the saints *with this chord progression, but beware of the different lengths of upbeats* — When the saints *will need to start first.*

- Work out the tune by ear.
- Say the words in strict rhythm to find and underline the strong beats.
- Sing or hum the tune while you work out the chords and write in chord symbols beneath the lyrics.
- Write the chord progression in the boxes given.
- Practise it hands together, listening rather than looking at the book.

Right-hand five-finger position

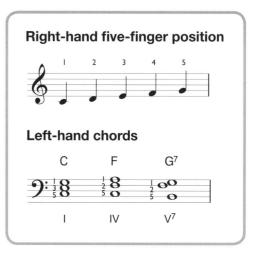

Left-hand chords

Jingle bells (begins on E)

3

Jingle bells, jingle bells, jingle all the way,

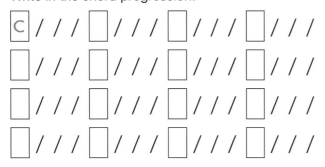

Oh what fun it is to ride in a one-horse open sleigh, hey!

Jingle bells, jingle bells, jingle all the way,

Oh what fun it is to ride in a one-horse open sleigh.

Clash

Write in the chord progression:

C	/ / /		/ / /		/ / /		/ / /
	/ / /		/ / /		/ / /		/ / /
	/ / /		/ / /		/ / /		/ / /
	/ / /		/ / /		/ / /		/ / /

Tip

If you write the chords in Roman numerals you will be able to play the progression in different keys very easily.

Accompanying *Happy Birthday*

Write in the words to *Happy birthday* on the two lines below.

- Find and underline the strong beats.
- Sing or hum the tune while you work out the chords.
- Write the chord progression in the boxes provided.
- Practise the progression first in block chords and then in the waltz rhythm below.

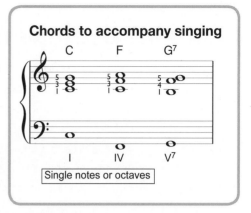

Chords to accompany singing

Single notes or octaves

Tip — To encourage everyone to sing, play the key-chord (C major) warmly and firmly, then the starting note, G, as a left-hand 'drumroll' octave to bring everyone in.

Happy Birthday
(begins on the G below middle C)

Upbeat

Happy birthday_____ , _____

_____ , _____

Write in the chord progression:

Upbeat / ☐ / / ☐ / / ☐ / / ☐ /

/ ☐ / / ☐ / / ☐ / ☐ ☐ / Extra chord

Waltz rhythm accompaniment

Happy birthday is a celebratory song in three time, so you could play the chords in this rousing waltz rhythm. You will need to fill in the missing chords.

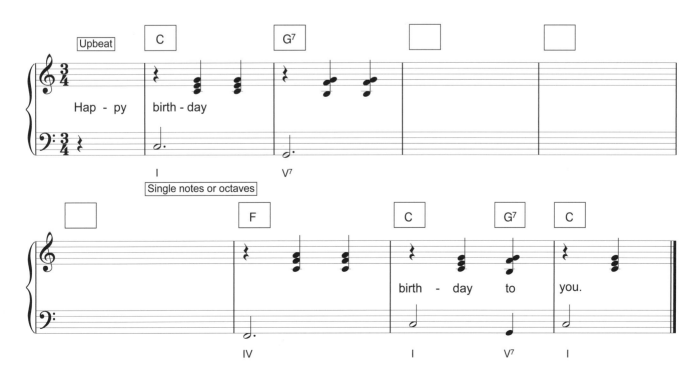

29

Looking at phrasing

Phrases are generally named with letters and often paired as 'questions' and 'answers'. The first phrase is always called A. If the second phrase is the same as the first it is also called A. If it's different, it's called B, and so on. The phrase pattern of *Mary had a little lamb* is ABAC, and it's easy to work out because the musical phrases are reflected by the lyrics (they aren't always). The musical phrases are also reflected by the lyrics in *Do wah diddy diddy*, and the first four phrases are very similar so they're easy to play by ear.

- Sing the song and work out the phrase pattern.
- Then work out the tune and chords, and play hands together.

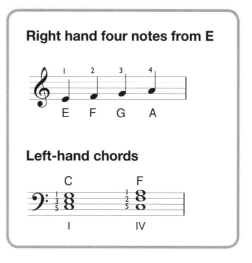

Right hand four notes from E

Left-hand chords

Do wah diddy diddy

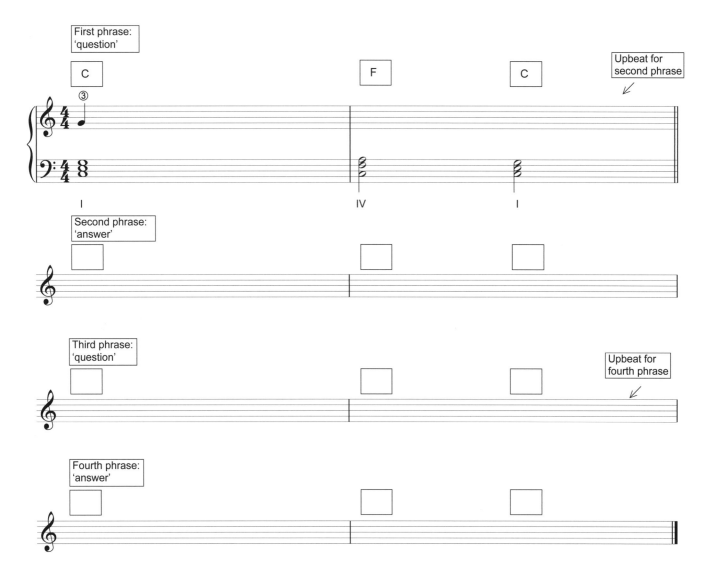

Using five white notes and two chords

The five notes C D E G A form the C pentatonic scale. It is more comfortable to play them in the order G A C D E. Pentatonic scales are wonderful for improvising as they never sound 'wrong'.

- Practise the right-hand notes and the left-hand chords separately.
- Set a steady pulse, and play the four-bar left-hand introduction to set the mood.
- Then improvise four phrases simply and naturally. You can think in questions and answers, phrase patterns (ABAC or ABCB etc.) or improvise freely.

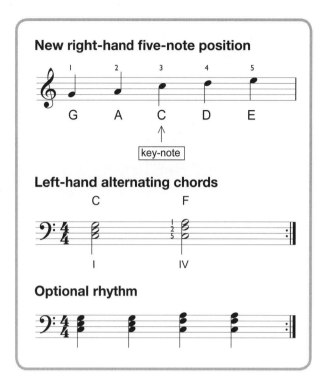

New right-hand five-note position

G   A   C   D   E

key-note

Left-hand alternating chords

C   F

I   IV

Optional rhythm

At the end of the day

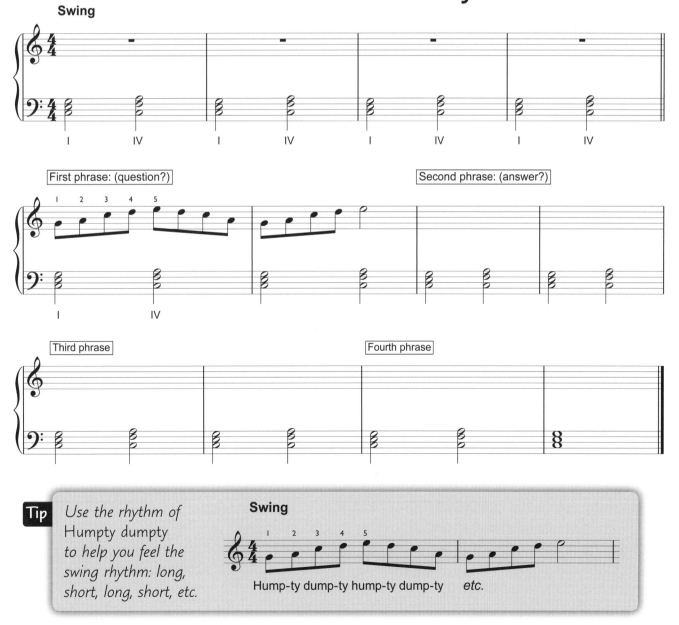

Swing

I   IV   I   IV   I   IV   I   IV

First phrase: (question?)   Second phrase: (answer?)

I   IV

Third phrase   Fourth phrase

Tip *Use the rhythm of Humpty dumpty to help you feel the swing rhythm: long, short, long, short, etc.*

Swing

Hump-ty dump-ty hump-ty dump-ty   *etc.*

Adding a blue note

The E♭ gives this right-hand five-note position a cool, 'bluesy' sound.

- Practise the right-hand notes and the left-hand chords separately.
- Set a steady pulse and play the four-bar left-hand introduction to set the mood.
- Then improvise four two-bar phrases.
- As the improvisation is in 3-time it can help to think in the rhythm of a 3-time song. The suggested opening uses the rhythm of *Lavender's Blue*.

Right-hand five-note position with E flat

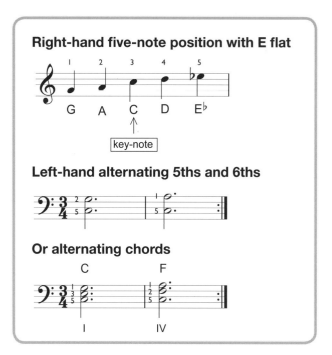

Left-hand alternating 5ths and 6ths

Or alternating chords

Wild flower meadow

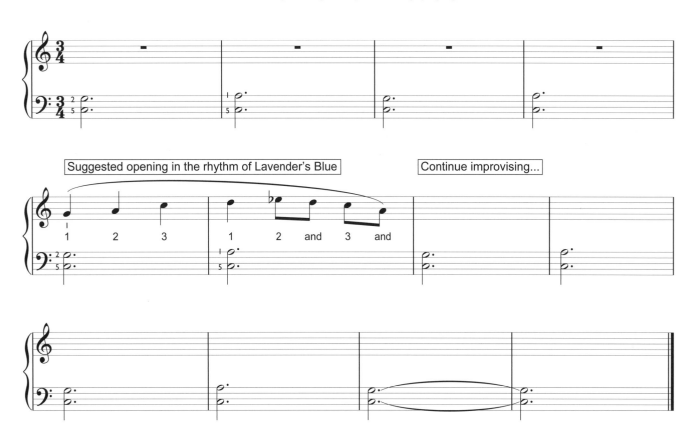

Suggested opening in the rhythm of Lavender's Blue

Continue improvising...

 Tip

If you memorise the left-hand chord patterns and right-hand positions you will be able to improvise anytime, anywhere!

Using five notes and three chords

- Practise the right-hand notes and left-hand chords separately.
- Set a steady pulse and play the eight-bar (repeated) left-hand introduction.
- Then improvise four four-bar phrases.
- It can help to think in the rhythm of a 4-time song. The suggested opening uses the rhythm of *London Bridge*.

Right hand five-note position with optional E♭

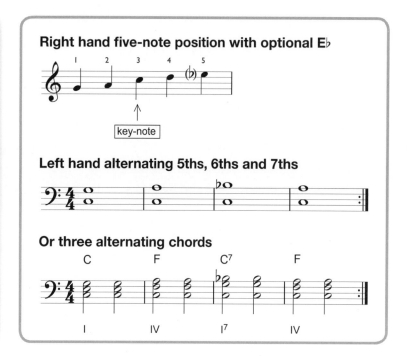

Left hand alternating 5ths, 6ths and 7ths

Or three alternating chords

A night on the town

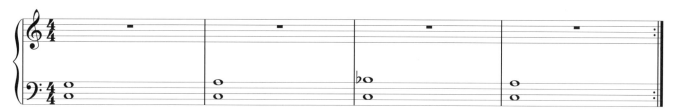

Suggested opening in the rhythm of London Bridge

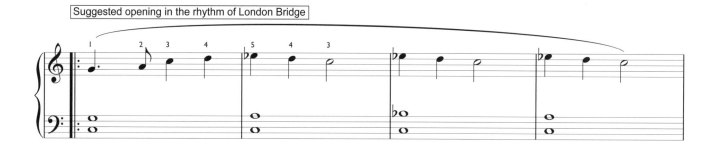

Continue improvising...

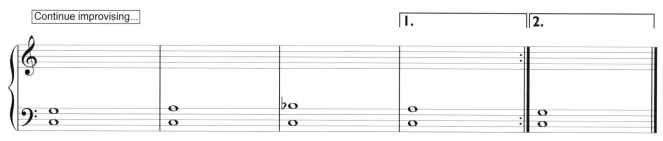

Repeat the left-hand and continue improvising. End on the keychord, C.

Tip *Repeating in different octaves is a simple and effective way to extend an improvisation. Try repeating one octave higher, then return to the original octave for the third and final time.*

Playing six-note tunes

- Play the six-note position with the two fingerings given.
- Practise the right hand of *Jolly good fellow*, noticing the suggested fingering.
- Sing or hum the tune while you work out the chords and write in the chord symbols.
- Practise hands together without looking at the book.

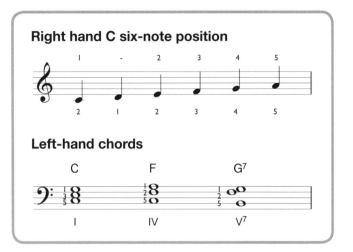

Right hand C six-note position

Left-hand chords

Jolly good fellow

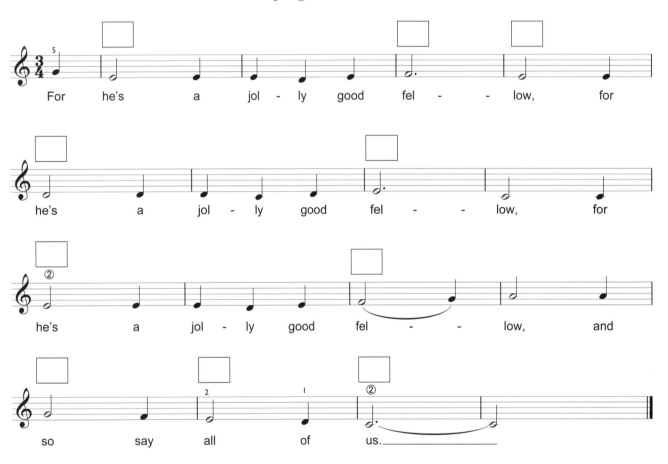

For he's a jol - ly good fel - - low, for

he's a jol - ly good fel - - low, for

he's a jol - ly good fel - - low, and

so say all of us.

Tip

A strong accompaniment both inspires and supports singers.

Similar songs

I'm gonna sing, sing, sing (begins on E)
The lion sleeps tonight (begins on C)
   from *The lion king*
Whistle while you work (begins on G)
   from *Snow White*

Six-note tunes in 3-time

- All the tunes on this page have the same phrase pattern: ABAC.
- Work out the tune and chord progression in the usual way, finding the most sensible and consistent fingering, and a simple but musically satisfying chord progression.
- You can write in any notes, fingering and chord symbols to help you.

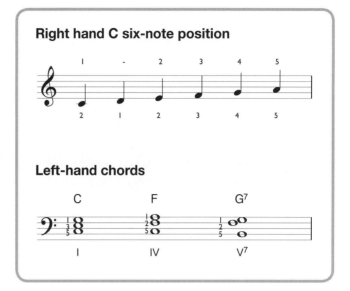

Right hand C six-note position

Left-hand chords

Lavender's blue
(begins on C)

Lavender's blue, dilly dilly,

Lavender's green,

When you are king, dilly dilly,

I shall be queen.

Pop goes the weasel
(begins on C)

Half a pound of tuppenny rice,

Half a pound of treacle,

That's the way the money goes,

Pop! Goes the weasel.

Kum-ba-yah
(begins on C)

Kum-ba-ya my Lord, Kum-ba-yah!

Kum-ba-ya my Lord, Kum-ba-yah!

Kum-ba-ya my Lord, Kum-ba-yah!

Oh, Lord, Kum-ba-yah!

Tip

Aim to listen and to look at your hands rather than the book, to be able to play anytime, anywhere.

Six-note tunes in 4-time

Work out the tune and chord progression in the usual way, finding the most sensible and consistent fingering, and a simple but musically satisfying chord progression. You can write in any notes, fingering and chord symbols to help you.

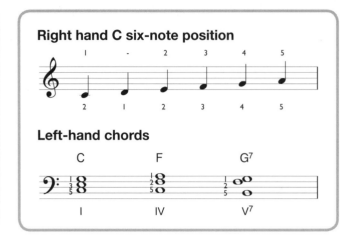

Right hand C six-note position

Left-hand chords

London Bridge
(begins on G)

London Bridge is falling down,

Falling down, falling down,

London Bridge is falling down,

My fair lady.

This old man
(begins on G)

This old man, he played one,

He played knick-knack on my thumb,

With a knick-knack paddy-whack, give a dog a bone,

This old man came rolling home.

Michael, row the boat
(begins on C)

Michael, row the boat ashore,

Al-le-lu-jah!

Michael, row the boat ashore,

Al-le-lu-u-jah!

Twinkle, twinkle little star
(begins on C)

Twinkle, twinkle, little star,

How I wonder what you are,

Up above the world so high,

Like a diamond in the sky,

Twinkle, twinkle, little star,

How I wonder what you are.

Similar songs with six notes from B to G
Mary Ann (begins on E)
Polly wolly doodle (begins on C)
Skip to my Lou (begins on E)

Similar song with seven notes from B to A
Blowing in the wind Bob Dylan (begins on G)

Pentatonic tunes in C

You may have realised that the tunes you played on black notes at the start were pentatonic. There are two main pentatonic positions:

1 Root position: CDE GA (or F♯G♯A♯ C♯D♯ on black notes).

2 Inverted: GA CDE (or C♯D♯ F♯G♯A♯).

The inverted position is comfortable, but when playing in root position it's helpful to use the six-note tune fingering.

Play and harmonise the pentatonic tunes below in the usual way.

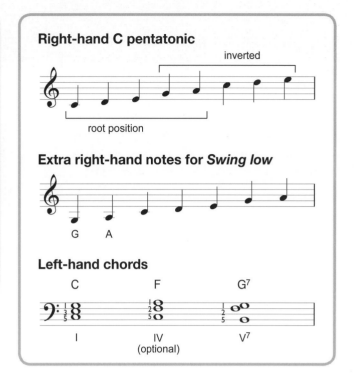

Right-hand C pentatonic

Extra right-hand notes for *Swing low*

Left-hand chords

Oh Susanna (begins on C)

I come from Alabama

With my banjo on my knee

I'm going to Louisiana,

Susanna for to see.

Camptown races (begins on G)

The Camptown ladies sing this song,

Doo-da, doo-da,

The Camptown racetrack's five miles long

Oh, doo-da day.

Swing low, sweet chariot

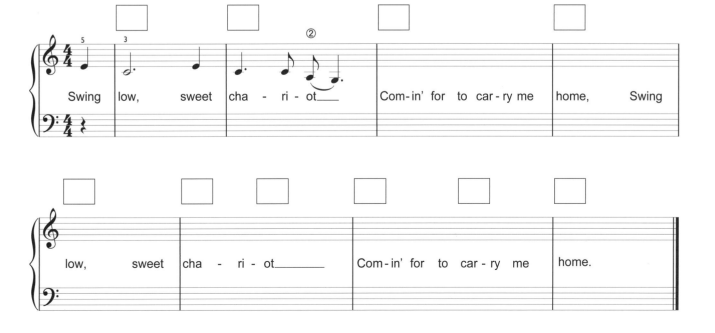

Playing in G major

To create the sound of a major scale when beginning in G you will need an F♯.
The F♯ appears as a **key signature** to remind you to play F♯ throughout.
Here are the primary chords in G major in root position:

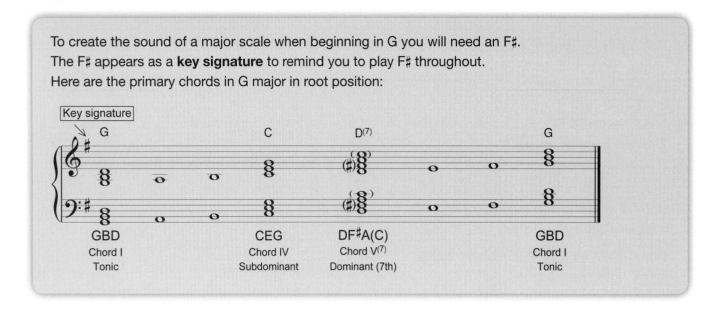

A grand arpeggio progression

- Practise the new chord, D major, as a grand arpeggio.
- Remember to use the pedal.
- Then play the four-chord progression: G, C, D, G in grand arpeggios.
- You will need to change the pedal for each grand arpeggio.

G major primary chords in comfortable inversions

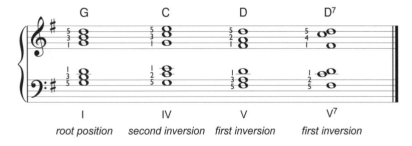

A G major broken chord progression

Now practise these inversions as broken chords. If you used consistent fingering when playing this in C major you will find it easy. Listen carefully, and remember to play F♯.

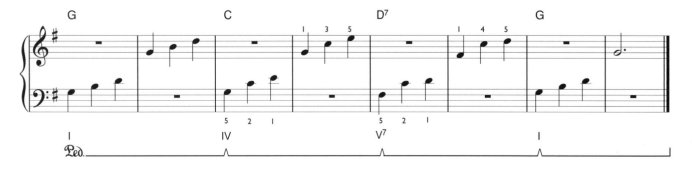

Transposing from C to G major

Choose a song that you have already played in C major and play it in G major.
This is called **transposing**: a very useful musical skill. Here are some to try:

Mary had a little lamb

(begins on B)

Mary had a little lamb,

Little lamb, little lamb,

Mary had a little lamb,

Its fleece was white as snow.

Right-hand G five-finger position

G A B C D

Left-hand chords

G   D   D⁷

I   V   or   V⁷

One man went to mow

(begins on B)

One man went to mow,

Went to mow a meadow,

One man and his dog,

Went to mow a meadow.

Kum-ba-yah (begins on G)

Kum-ba-ya my Lord, Kum-ba-yah!

Kum-ba-ya my Lord, Kum-ba-yah!

Kum-ba-ya my Lord, Kum-ba-yah!

Oh, Lord, Kum-ba-yah!

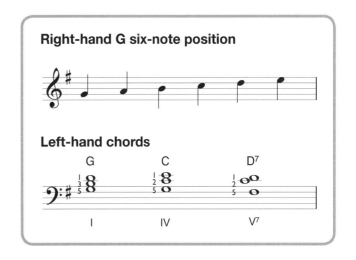

Right-hand G six-note position

Left-hand chords

G   C   D⁷

I   IV   V⁷

For he's a jolly good fellow

(begins on D)

For he's a jolly good fellow,

For he's a jolly good fellow,

For he's a jolly good fellow,

And so say all of us.

Changing key within a song

- In *Oranges and lemons* you will need to change key (and hand position) for one phrase. Changing key within a piece is called **modulating**.
- Sing the song first and work out where this change is. You will need to move down to play it.
- Write the chord progression in the boxes given.

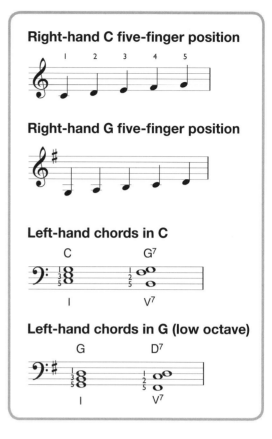

Right-hand C five-finger position

Right-hand G five-finger position

Left-hand chords in C

Left-hand chords in G (low octave)

Similar songs to try in either C or G major

Ring o' roses (begins on F, or C, with Chord V)
Bye baby Bunting (begins on F, or C, Chord V)
Girls and boys (begins on G, or D)

Oranges and lemons (begins with 5 on G)

Oranges and lemons say the bells of St Clements,

You owe me five farthings say the bells of St Martins,

When will you pay me say the bells of Old Bailey?

When I grow rich say the bells of Shoreditch.

Improvising with broken-chord progressions

Broken-chord progressions are very easy and provide an endless source of inspiration.

They can be played ascending:

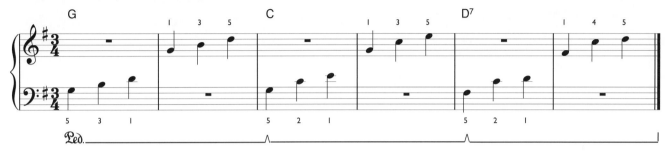

Or descending:

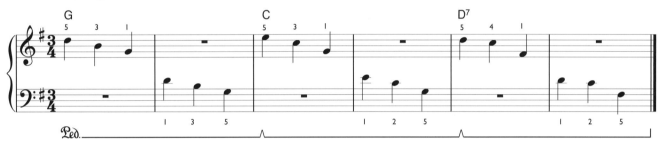

Over two, four or six octaves (begin as low as you want and continue up the piano):

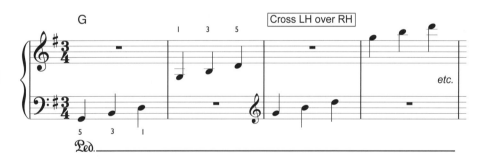

- Create your own progression using at least two of the three primary chords in G (G, C or D⁷).

- You can play the chords ascending or descending, over two, four or six octaves, using root position or inverted chords. End with the G chord.

- Then try this eight-chord progression in C major. It uses the primary chords in C major, and chords G and D⁷ – so there is a brief modulation to G major.

- Play each chord ascending, over four octaves, finishing with a single left-hand note, C.

C	F	D⁷	G
LH RH LH RH	LH RH LH RH	LH RH LH RH	LH RH LH RH

C	F	G⁷	C
LH RH LH RH	LH RH LH RH	LH RH LH RH	LH RH LH

Tip

Use your musical instinct to decide how to bring your broken-chord progression to an end.

41

Solo and group improvising in G

To play solo

- Choose one **left-hand idea** and one **right-hand position** and improvise in the usual way.

- Remember to set a steady pulse and play four left-hand bars as an introduction.

- Think in the rhythm of a 3-time song, use question and answer phrases and phrase repetition or improvise freely.

- Bring your improvisation to an end on the key-note and chord (G major).

To play with two or more people

- The leader must play a left-hand **repeated bass**. Everyone else can choose whether to play with one or both hands.

- The notes can be played in any octave, but be careful not to play the chords too low, as they will sound too 'thick'.

- The leader sets a steady pulse and guides left-hand players to enter at two-bar intervals. Then right-hand players enter, listening and responding to each other.

- Players can bring their own parts to an end individually, or be guided to a close on the key-note and chord (G major).

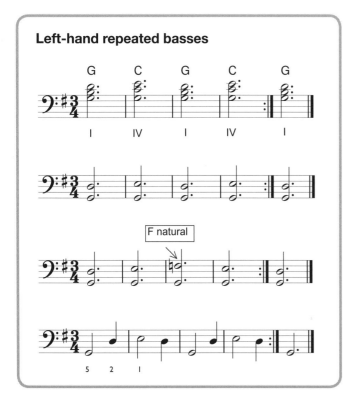

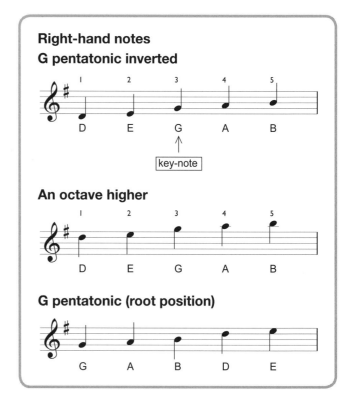

Tip

If playing solo, try playing B flat instead of B in the right hand. (The left must always play B natural). If playing with two or more people either B or B flat must be chosen and played consistently in both hands.

Introducing the twelve-bar blues

The **twelve-bar blues** is a very common chord progression in jazz and blues. This is the sequence of chords (one chord per bar):

I	I	I	I
IV	IV	I	I
V	IV	I	I

Off-beat rhythms

In jazz and blues the left hand drives the rhythm, and the right-hand's melodies (or 'licks') are often off-beat (**syncopated**).

- Practise the right-hand notes and left-hand progression separately.
- When secure, set a steady pulse and enjoy improvising.

Right-hand G pentatonic (inverted)

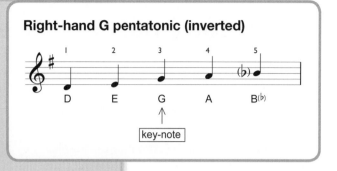

Twelve-bar blues in G

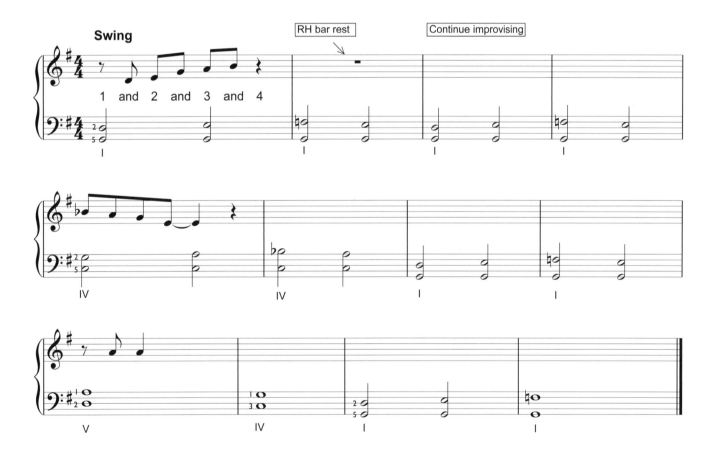

 Tip

The optional B♭ sounds best with chord IV (the C chord in this key).

Similar songs

Tutti frutti (begins on D) Penniman, La Bostre and Lubin
Johnny B. Goode (begins on G) Chuck Berry

Open 5th chords

Many popular songs can be harmonised with open 5th chords.

- Work out the tune and chords in the usual way.
- When completely secure improvise over the chord progression.

 Tip *Pop tunes do not always end on chord I, often they simply fade away.*

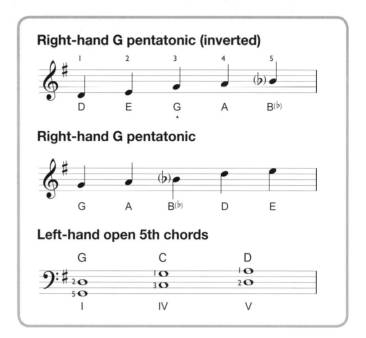

Right-hand G pentatonic (inverted)

Right-hand G pentatonic

Left-hand open 5th chords

Similar songs

That'll be the day that I die (begins on B♭)

Great balls of fire (begins on B♭)

Nine to five

Optional rhythm for repeated chords

rising bass line

Broken-chord accompaniments

You can vary the way chords are played to convey the character of the song. Here are some broken-chord progressions for a flowing and lyrical accompaniment.

First, play the usual broken-chord progression:

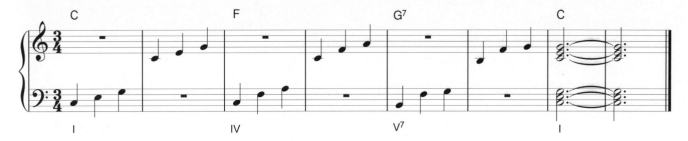

Then double the speed:

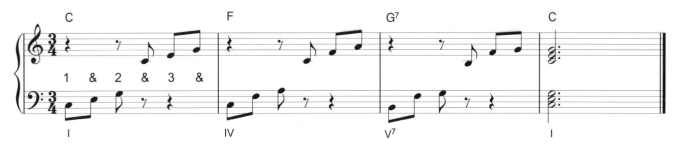

Now try with the root of the chord in your left hand:

Finally, with octave roots for a full and rich sound:

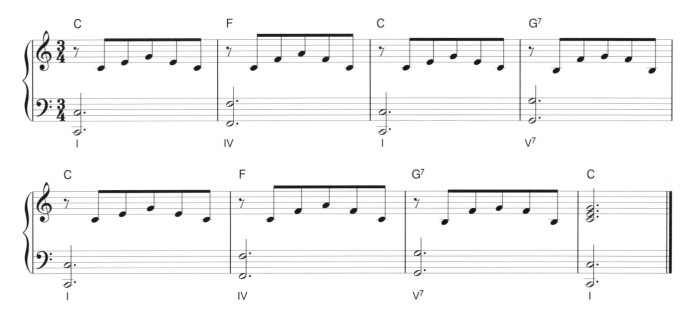

Accompanying Silent night

- Sing or hum the tune while you work out and write in the chord progression.
- Play the progression in block chords while you sing or hum the tune.
- Then try playing in broken chords to convey the gentle beauty of the lullaby.
- Each broken chord needs to be repeated, except for the quick change of chord at the end.
- Use your musical instinct to decide how to play the very last chord (or note).

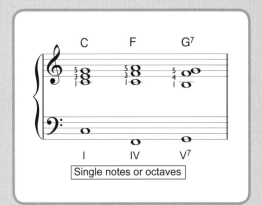

Silent night (begins on G)

Silent night, holy night, All is calm, all is bright

Round yon Virgin, Mother and Child, Holy Infant so tender and mild

Sleep in heavenly peace, Sleep in heavenly peace.

☐ / / / / / ☐ / / / / / ☐ / / / / / ☐ / / / / /

☐ / / / / / ☐ / / / / / ☐ / / / / / ☐ / / / / /

☐ / / / / / ☐ / / / / / ☐ / / ☐ / / ☐ / / / / /

Playing eight-note tunes

This tune covers an octave – all eight notes of the scale.

- Practise the right-hand scale, then play and complete the tune.
- Sing or hum the tune while you work out the chords, and put hands together.
- Try the broken chords to accompany singing.

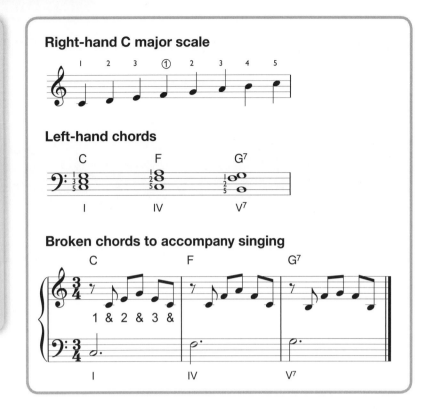

Right-hand C major scale

Left-hand chords

Broken chords to accompany singing

The first noel

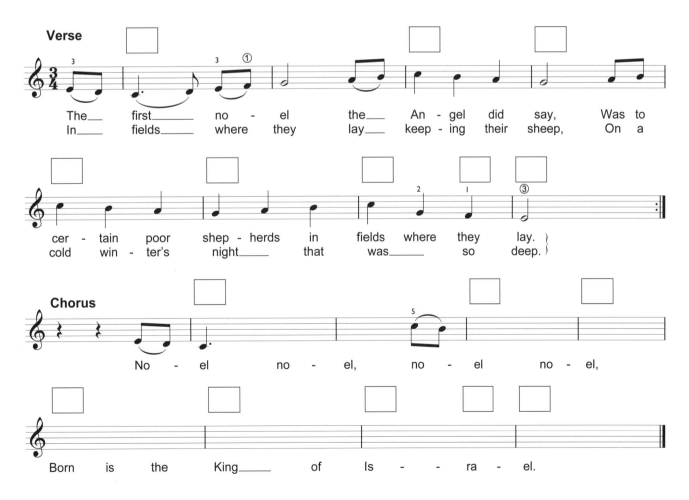

Verse

The___ first_____ no - el the___ An - gel did say, Was to
In___ fields_____ where they lay___ keep - ing their sheep, On a

cer - tain poor shep - herds in fields where they lay.
cold win - ter's night_____ that was_____ so deep.

Chorus

No - el no - el, no - el no - el,

Born is the King_____ of Is - - ra - el.

Similar songs/themes

Lullaby Brahms (begins on E)
Mr. Tambourine Man Bob Dylan (begins on C)

Tip *The verse and chorus are very similar.*

- Work out the tunes and chords in the usual way, with block chords.
- Try playing the left hand with broken chords when secure. They are very useful for filling the musical space when your right hand is playing long, held notes.

Right-hand C major scale

C major arpeggio

Left-hand chords

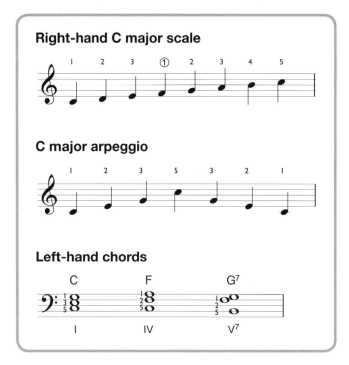

Row the boat (begins on C)

Row, row, row your boat,

Gently down the stream,

Merrily, merrily, merrily, merrily,

Life is but a dream.

Tip

Music does not always begin on chord I.

Similar songs

Baa baa black sheep (begins on C)
Hickory dickory dock (begins on E)
Three blind mice (begins on E)

On top of Old Smokey (begins on C)

Repeat the chord here:

On top of Old Smokey _____, All covered with snow _____,

I lost my true lover _____, From a-courtin' too slow _____,

For courtin's a pleasure _____, And partin' is grief _____,

A false hearted lover _____, Is worse than a thief _____.

The range of a song

The **range** of a song is the distance from the lowest to highest note. The range of *Joy to the world* is an octave, from middle C to the C above (C–C').

- Work out the tune and chords for *Joy to the world* in the usual way. There is one chord per bar, except where indicated.

Similar songs

Lily the Pink (begins on G)

Flintstones theme (begins on G)

Can-can from *Orpheus in the underworld* Offenbach (begins on C)

English country garden (begins on C, range C–D')

Where have all the flowers gone Pete Seeger (begins on G, range C–D')

Imagine John Lennon (begins on G, range E–G')

Right-hand C major scale

Left-hand chords

Chords to accompany singing

Joy to the world

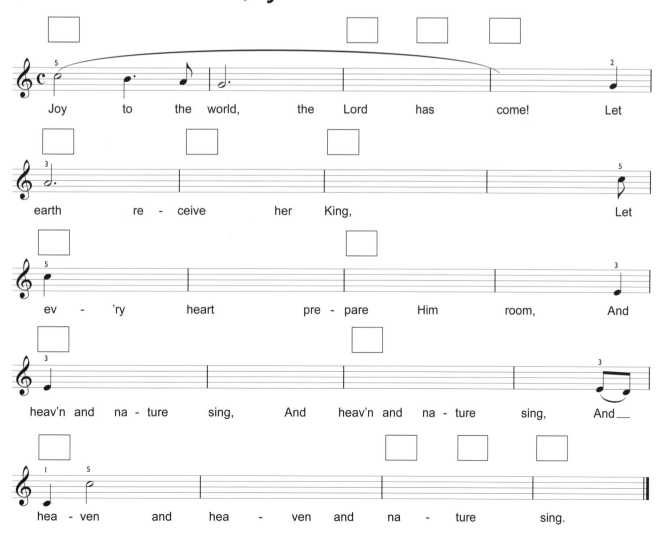

49

Calypso

Calypso comes from the Caribbean, and has a distinctive quaver rhythm, emphasising the first, fourth and seventh quavers of each bar.

- Practise the two calypso accompaniments below, counting in quavers.
- Then try it while you sing or hum the tune.
- You can also try the right-hand tune with one held left-hand chord per bar.

Similar songs

The banana boat song
   Traditional Jamaican (3rd)
Jamaica farewell
   (5th includes the F chord)

Water come a me eye

Playing in F major

To create the sound of a major scale when beginning on F you will need a B♭. The B♭ appears as a **key signature** to remind you to play B♭ instead of B throughout. Here are the primary chords in F major in root position:

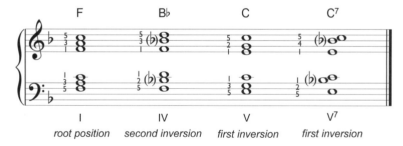

A grand arpeggio progression

- Practise the new chord, B♭ as a grand arpeggio. Use the usual fingering, even though it includes a black note.
- Remember to use the pedal.
- Then play a four-chord grand arpeggio progression: F, B♭, C, F. Remember to change the pedal for each grand arpeggio.

F major primary chords in comfortable inversions

Play a broken-chord progression

Now practise this F major broken-chord progression. If you used consistent fingering when you played the C and G major progressions, you will find it easy. Listen carefully, and be aware of the B flats!

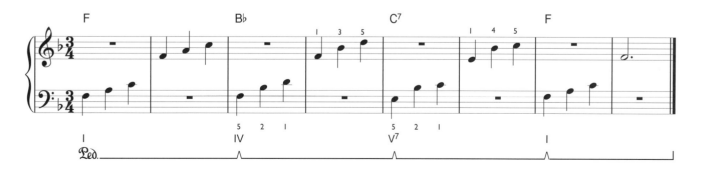

Transposing from C to F major

Choose a song that you have already played in C major and play it in F major. See if you can 'hear' and find the starting note without looking it up.

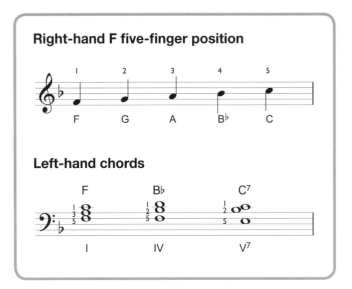

Right-hand F five-finger position

F G A B♭ C

Left-hand chords

F   B♭   C⁷

I   IV   V⁷

One man went to mow

One man went to mow,

Went to mow a meadow,

One man and his dog,

Went to mow a meadow.

Jingle bells chorus

Jingle bells, jingle bells, jingle all the way,

Oh what fun it is to ride in a one horse open sleigh, hey!

Jingle bells, jingle bells, jingle all the way,

Oh what fun it is to ride in a one horse open sleigh.

Oranges and lemons

Remember that you need to change key within this song. The second key is one you know well!

Oranges and lemons say the bells of St Clements,

You owe me five farthings say the bells of St Martins,

When will you pay me say the bells of Old Bailey?

When I grow rich say the bells of Shoreditch.

Similar songs

Look back through the book and try any other songs you like!

More open 5th chords

Open 5th chords were used in Medieval and Renaissance music and sound very effective with this ancient carol.

Work out the tune and open 5th chords in the usual way.

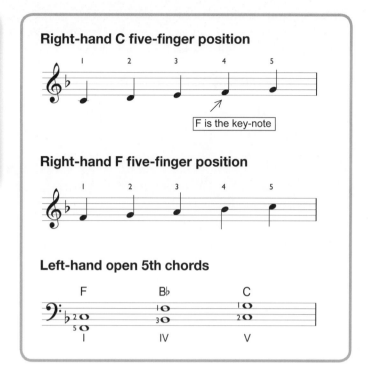

Right-hand C five-finger position

F is the key-note

Right-hand F five-finger position

Left-hand open 5th chords

F   Bb   C

I   IV   V

Good King Wenceslas

(begins on F with finger 4)

Good King Wenceslas looked out

On the feast of Stephen,

When the snow lay round about,

Deep and crisp and even,

| Change to the F position | Brightly shone the moon that night |

| Change position | Though the frost was cruel, |

When a poor man came in <u>sight</u>   Optional C chord (V)

| Change position | Gath'ring winter fu-el. |

Similar songs

Ten little Indians (begins on F)
Frère Jacques (begins on F, range C-D')

A popular three-chord progression

F / / / F / / / F / / / C⁷ / / /
F / / / B♭/ / / F / C⁷ / F / / /

The following songs can be sung individually or simultaneously with others to this progression.
When the saints (begins on F)
I'm gonna sing (begins on A)
She'll be comin' (begins on C)
Swing low (begins on A)
This train (begins on F)

To sing simultaneously:

- Practise the progression, then sing or hum your chosen songs in turn to find the pulse (speed) that suits them all, as you play.
- Decide who is going to sing which song, and their order of entry. Songs can enter one at a time, a verse apart or simultaneously. If entering simultaneously take care with the different upbeats: songs with the longest upbeat enter first, so they all arrive on the downbeat together.

The usual right-hand chords may sound too high in F major

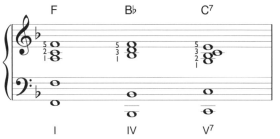

Alternative right-hand chord positions

Oh when the <u>Saints</u> (begins on F)

   I'm gonna <u>sing</u>, sing, sing (begins on A)

      She'll be <u>comin'</u> round the mountain (begins on C)

         Swing <u>low</u>, sweet chariot (begins on A)

            <u>This</u> train is bound for glory (begins on F)

Downbeat

March rhythm accompaniment

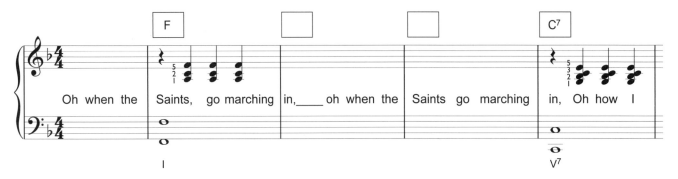

Avoiding overlapping hands

Tunes often begin on the lower dominant (four notes below the tonic). When right-hand notes below the tonic are needed, the top left-hand chord notes can be omitted and the position of the chords can change to avoid overlapping hands.

Notice that the usual top note has been omitted from chords I and IV, and chord V⁷ is in root position as an open 7th.

Work out the tune and chords in the usual way, and then try it hands together. You usually need two chords per bar.

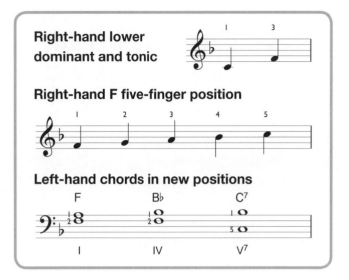

Right-hand lower dominant and tonic

Right-hand F five-finger position

Left-hand chords in new positions

Similar songs

Ten in a bed (begins on low C)
Michael Finnigan (begins on low C)
Yankee doodle (begins on F)

London's burning

Lon-don's burn - ing, Lon-don's burn - ing, Fetch the en - gine, fetch the en - gine, Fire,

fire! Fire, fire! Pour on wa - ter, pour on wa - ter.

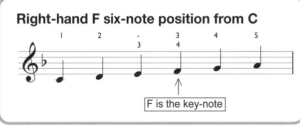

Right-hand F six-note position from C

F is the key-note

There's a hole in my bucket

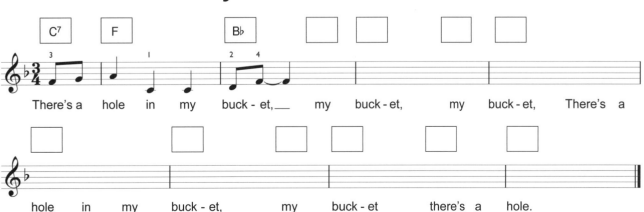

There's a hole in my buck - et,___ my buck - et, my buck - et, There's a

hole in my buck - et, my buck - et there's a hole.

Playing *Happy birthday*

F major is perhaps the most comfortable key to sing *Happy birthday* in: neither too high for adults nor too low for children.

- Write the words in the space provided, noticing the four phrases.
- Underline the strong beats and work out the chord progression.
- Then work out the tune, and practise until you can play without looking at the book.
- Fill in the missing chords to play the whole accompaniment to *Happy birthday*. Notice the second inversion of the F major chord in the penultimate bar.

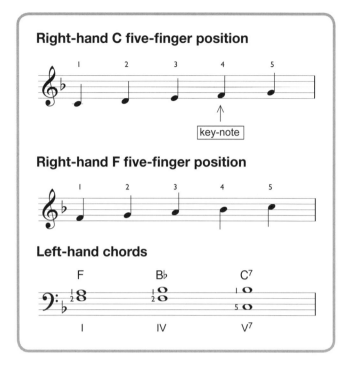

Right-hand C five-finger position

Right-hand F five-finger position

Left-hand chords

Happy birthday

<u>Happy birthday</u> , _____

_____ , _____

Similar songs to try

If you're happy and you know it

Waltz rhythm accompaniment

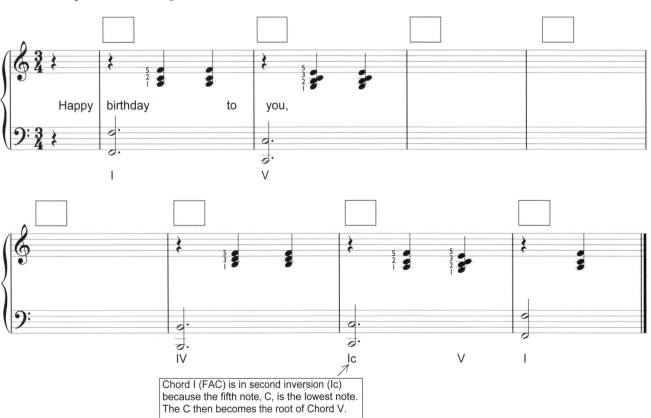

Happy | birthday | to | you,

Chord I (FAC) is in second inversion (Ic) because the fifth note, C, is the lowest note. The C then becomes the root of Chord V.

Here are two more songs in F major to try. They use more notes in the tune so you will need to take care with your fingering. Notice that *I saw three ships* starts on the dominant of F major.

Right-hand F major from the dominant

Left-hand chords

Chords to accompany singing

Similar songs

I saw three ships (alternative version)

I   saw   three   ships   come   sail - ing   in

Quem pastores (begins on F)
On Christmas night (begins on C)

I saw three ships

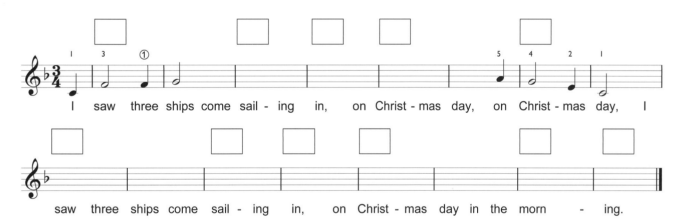

I   saw   three   ships   come   sail - ing   in,   on   Christ - mas   day,   on   Christ - mas   day,   I

saw   three   ships   come   sail - ing   in,   on   Christ - mas   day   in   the   morn   -   ing.

The holly and the ivy

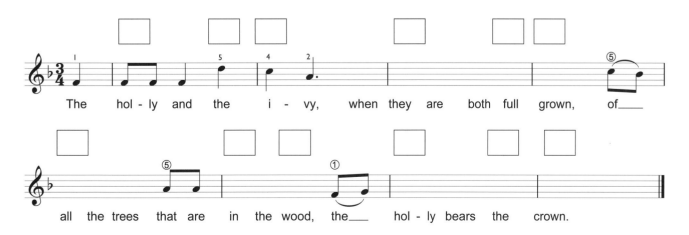

The   hol - ly   and   the   i - vy,   when   they   are   both   full   grown,   of____

all   the   trees   that   are   in   the   wood,   the____   hol - ly   bears   the   crown.

More accompaniment options in F major

You can try playing *Auld lang syne* in a variety of ways: with left-hand chords or open 5ths accompanying the right-hand tune, or with chords to accompany singing. You can also accompany this song with an open 5th on the key-note throughout, giving a sound reminiscent of the drone of Scottish bagpipes. Try out the different options and see which you prefer.

• Work out the tune and chords in the usual way. There is one chord per bar except where indicated.

Similar songs

Loch Lomond (begins on middle C and includes B♭, although mostly pentatonic)

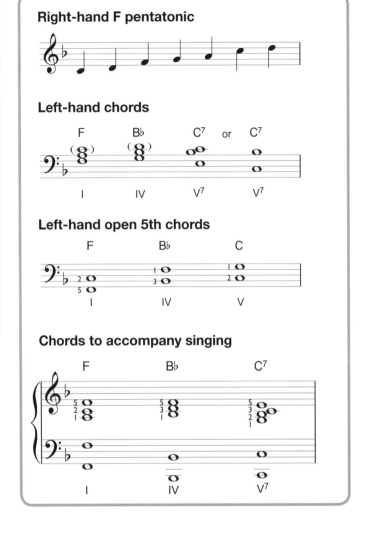

Right-hand F pentatonic

Left-hand chords

Left-hand open 5th chords

Chords to accompany singing

Auld lang syne

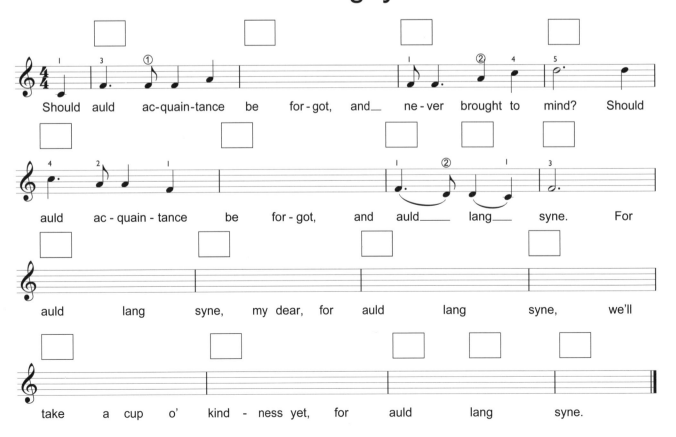

Should auld ac-quain-tance be for-got, and ne-ver brought to mind? Should

auld ac-quain-tance be for-got, and auld lang syne. For

auld lang syne, my dear, for auld lang syne, we'll

take a cup o' kind-ness yet, for auld lang syne.

Finding the starting note yourself

- Choose a tune and play the primary chords in F to tune you in, and help you hear the starting note.
- Find the starting note that you 'hear' inside your head on the piano.
- Work out the tune and chords in the usual way, choosing either full left-hand chords or open 5ths.

Songs to try

Li'l Liza Jane
Mary had a baby
Mull of Kintyre Wings
Nobody knows the trouble I've seen
Oh Susanna
Old Macdonald
Swing low sweet chariot
The Camptown Races
This train is bound for glory
Tom Dooley

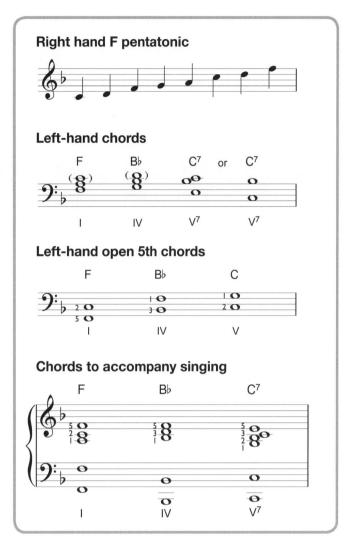

Right hand F pentatonic

Left-hand chords

Left-hand open 5th chords

Chords to accompany singing

 Tip It is easiest to work out pentatonic tunes on the black notes, playing F# instead of F and so on. You could then accompany them with open 5ths on F#.

Go, tell it on the mountain

Go, tell it on the mountain

Over the hills and everywhere

Go, tell ion the mountain

That Jesus Christ is born.

While shepherds kept their watching

Over silent flocks by night,

Behold throughout the heavens

There shone a holy light.

I'd like to teach the world to sing

I'd like to build the world a home

And furnish it with love,

Grow apple trees and honey bees

And snow-white turtle doves.

I'd like to teach the world to sing

In perfect harmony,

I'd like to hold it in my arms

And keep it company.

Working out the chords first

Now you're familiar with chords you'll find it's helpful to work them out first.

- Work out the chords, then the tune and write in the chord symbols. Put hands together or just play the chords to accompany singing.
- Try to work out the starting notes of the similar songs below. Play the primary chords in F to tune you in and help you hear the starting note.

Similar songs to try

Ten green bottles
Lord of the dance
Scooby Doo theme
Seasons in the sun Terry Jacks
I have a dream from *Mamma Mia*
One day like this (Elbow)

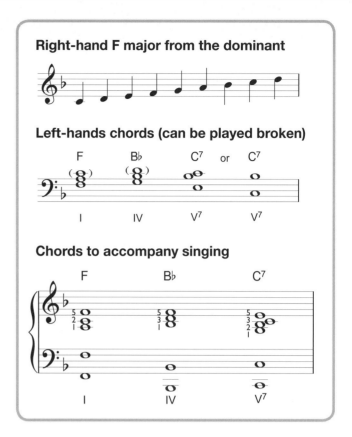

Tip *The phrase pattern is A A B A.*

O little town of Bethlehem

O lit - tle town of Beth - le - hem how still we see thee lie, A -

- bove thy deep and dream - less sleep the si - lent stars go by. But

in thy dark streets shi - - neth the e - ver - last - ing light, The

hopes and fears of all the years are met in thee to - night.

Improvising your own eight bars

- Create an eight-bar chord progression in the space below and write in the chord symbols. End the first half with an **imperfect cadence** (any chord followed by chord V), and the second half with a **perfect cadence**: chord V$^{(7)}$ to I, as shown.
- Then practise your progression in broken chords, experimenting until you have found a style that you like and can play fluently, as a beautiful composition.
- Finally, play the chords (blocked or broken) in your left hand, and improvise with your right hand.

Tip

It's easier to improvise with pentatonic than major scales. If you choose the major scale, listen carefully and consider which melody notes harmonise with which chords.

Right-hand F pentatonic with optional A♭

Best five-finger position for improvising

Right-hand F major scale

Left-hand chords (can be played broken)

Root position octave chords (can be played broken)

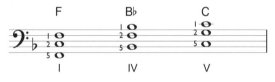

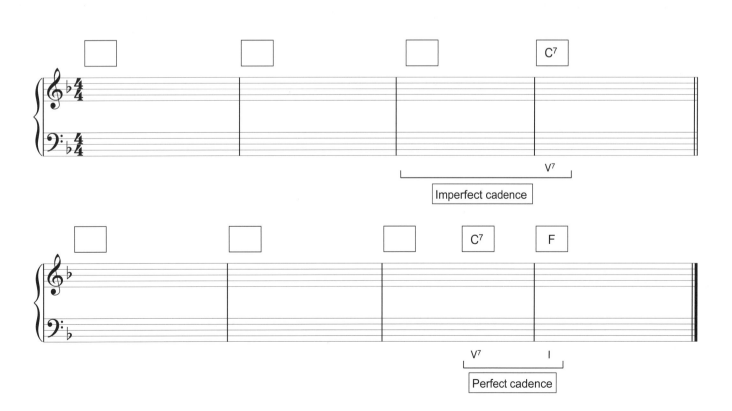

Walking bass

A **walking bass** outlines the chord progression in single notes. It is played by the double bass in a jazz group, or the left hand on a piano. There are many possible variations, two of which are shown here. As the main interest is in the left hand, the right hand need only play occasional off-beat chords.

- Complete and practise *Twelve-bar blues in F* walking bass below.
- When you're confident, add the off-beat right-hand chords.
- Then try the alternative walking bass style and off-beat chords and see which you prefer.

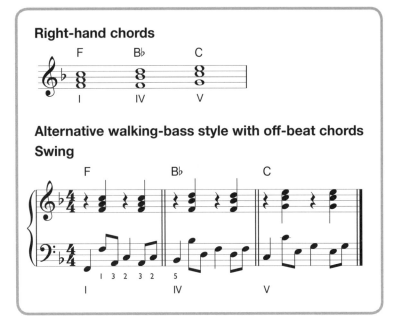

Similar song

The chorus of *Greased lightnin'* from *Grease* can be sung to this walking-bass accompaniment. Try it in F major (as shown) or transpose to C major to sing at a higher pitch (it begins on the key-note).

Twelve-bar blues in F

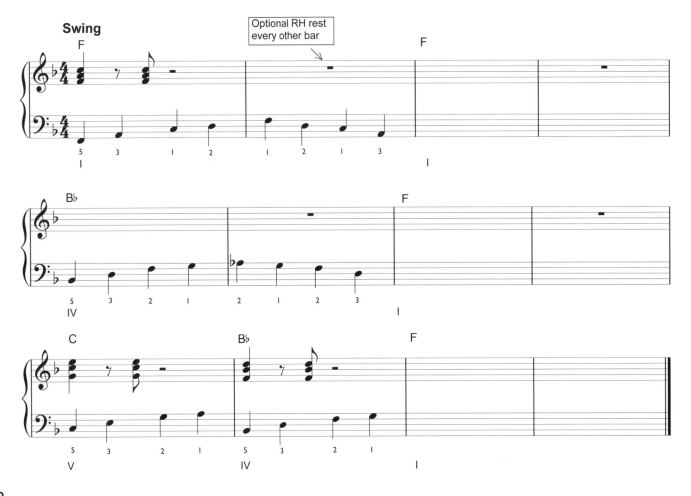

The pentatonic minor

Play the five black notes from E♭ to D♭ (D♯ to C♯) and you have found the pentatonic minor scale. (The pentatonic major scale is the five black notes from F♯ to D♯, or G♭ to E♭.)

- This haunting Canadian folk song is in the pentatonic minor.
- Learn it with the accompaniment of your choice.
- Then improvise over your accompaniment inspired by the rhythm, phrases and character of the song.

Right-hand black notes from E♭ (pentatonic minor)

Left-hand repeated basses open 5th chords (held or played in this rhythm)

Alternating tonic and dominant

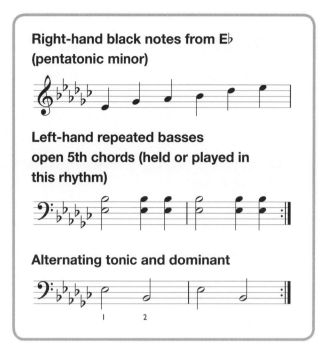

Land of the silver birch on black notes

Land of the sil - ver birch, home of the bea - ver, where still the might - y moose

wan-ders at will, Blue lake and rock - y shore, there I'll re - turn once more,

Boom tid - dly a - ti, boom tid - dly a - ti, boom tid - dly a - ti boom.

 Focus on your left hand: a secure and rhythmic accompaniment is the key to improvising.

Similar song

The canoe song (begins on B♭).

Solo or group improvising on black notes

Notice the difference in sound between major and minor: the major pentatonic (black notes from F♯/G♭) has a brighter, outward looking sound. The minor (black notes from E♭ or D♯) feels more personal and intimate.

To play solo

- Choose one left-hand repeated bass and one right-hand position and improvise in the usual way.
- Remember to set a steady pulse and play four left-hand bars as an introduction.
- Bring your improvisation to an end on the key-note and chord (E♭ minor).

To play with two or more people

- The leader must play a left-hand repeated bass. Everyone else can choose whether to play with one or both hands.
- The leader sets a steady pulse and guides left-hand players to enter at two-bar intervals. Then right-hand players enter, listening and responding to each other.
- Players can bring their own parts to an end individually, or be guided to a close on the key-note and chord (E♭ minor).

Variations: left hands can be played with rhythmic variation within the 4-time structure, and all left hands can be adapted for improvisation in 3 time.

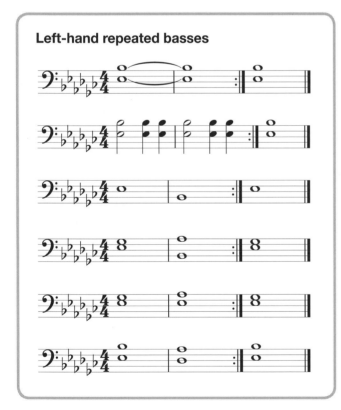

Left-hand repeated basses

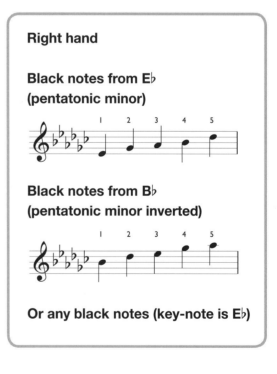

Right hand

Black notes from E♭ (pentatonic minor)

Black notes from B♭ (pentatonic minor inverted)

Or any black notes (key-note is E♭)

Tip

Remember that anyone (even non-piano players) can join in because all black notes can be played at once without sounding 'wrong'. Just maintain a steady pulse and rhythmic left hand, throughout.

Playing in A minor

Every major key has a **relative minor** that shares the same key signature. The relative minor of C major is A minor, so A minor has no sharps or flats in the key signature. However, in minor keys the seventh note of the scale is often sharpened with an accidental. So in A minor there is often a G sharp.

Here are the primary chords in A minor in root position:

Am	Dm	Em	E(7)	Am
ACE	DFA	EGB	EG#B(D)	ACE
Chord i	Chord iv	Chord v	Chord V(7)	Chord i
Tonic	Subdominant	Dominant	Dominant (7th)	Tonic

Minor chords and lower-case Roman numerals

Whether a chord is major or minor depends on the middle note (third). In major chords the middle note is a semitone higher than in minor chords. The fifth remains constant and is known as a perfect fifth.

Minor chords are indicated by lower case Roman numerals. So we would write chord i (A minor) and chord iv (D minor) in this key. Chord V (built on the fifth note of the scale) can be either minor or major depending on whether the seventh note of the scale is sharpened.

A grand arpeggio progression

Practise the A minor primary chords and then play them in a progression of grand arpeggios: Am, Dm, E, Am. Remember the G♯ accidental. You will need to change the pedal for each grand arpeggio.

A minor primary chords in comfortable inversions

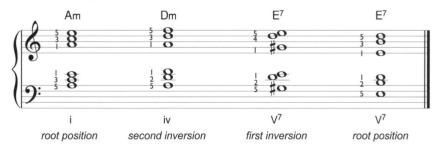

Am	Dm	E7	E7
i	iv	V7	V7
root position	*second inversion*	*first inversion*	*root position*

Open 5th chords in A minor

Practise these chords; you will find them very useful.

A	D	E	A	D	E
I	IV	V	I	IV	V

Open 5th chords provide easy and effective accompaniments for both major and minor keys because they are neither major nor minor themselves.

- Practise the A minor scale.
- Then play this old carol from Burgundy and harmonise it with open 5th chords.
- Finally, improvise over the chord progression, inspired by the rhythm, phrases and character of the song.

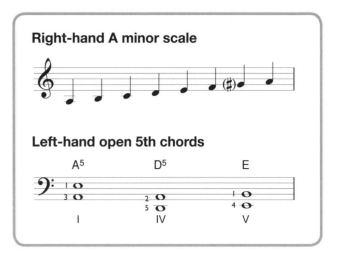

Right-hand A minor scale

Left-hand open 5th chords

Pat-a-pan

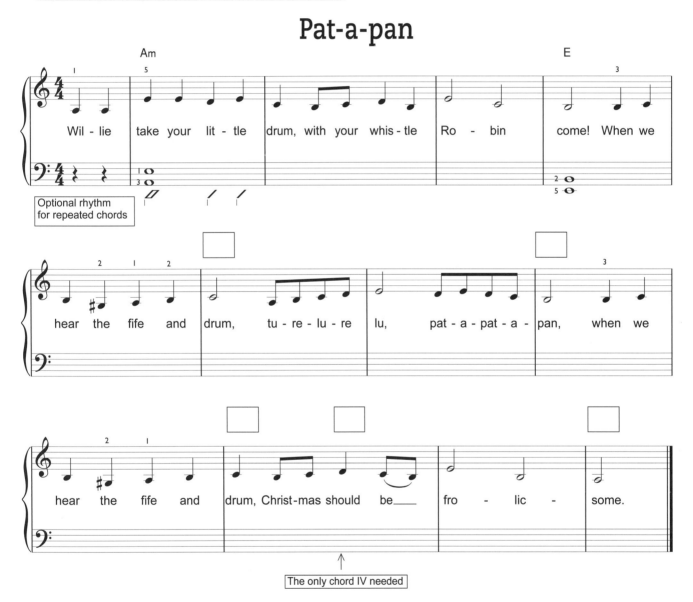

Wil - lie take your lit - tle drum, with your whis - tle Ro - bin come! When we

Optional rhythm for repeated chords

hear the fife and drum, tu - re - lu - re lu, pat - a - pat - a - pan, when we

hear the fife and drum, Christ-mas should be___ fro - lic - some.

The only chord IV needed

Suggested opening for improvisation, inverting the original melody

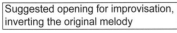
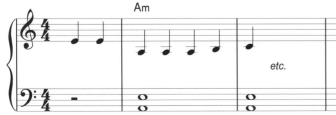

etc.

Similar song

The little drummer boy (begins on A) is in A major, so you will need some more sharps (your ear will guide you), but you can use the same open 5th chords.

Play and harmonise this evocative Russian folksong. Then improvise over the chord progression, decorating the existing melody with passing notes and rhythmic variations. An opening is suggested.

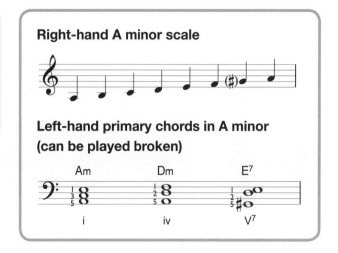

Song of the Volga boatmen

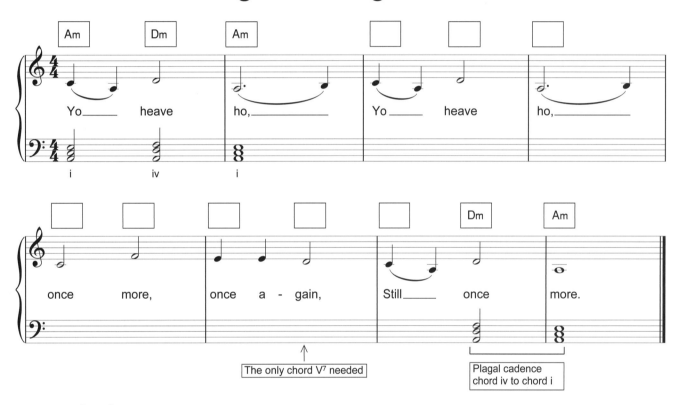

Improvisation

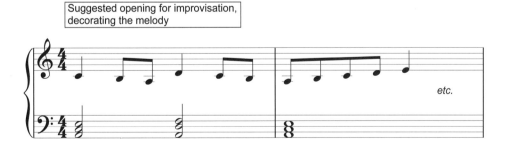

Similar tune

Hungarian dance no.4, first section, Brahms (begins on E)

Playing in E minor

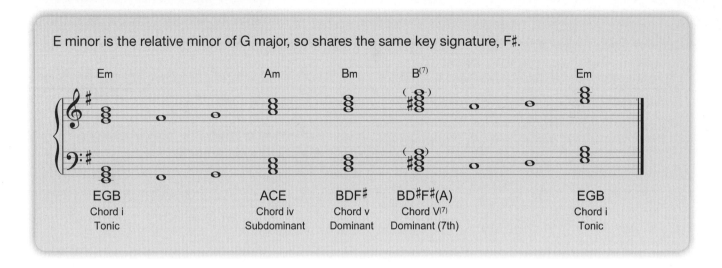

E minor is the relative minor of G major, so shares the same key signature, F♯.

A grand arpeggio progression

Practise the E minor primary chords and then play them in a progression of grand arpeggios: Em, Am, B and Em. Remember to include the D♯ accidental. Change the pedal for each grand arpeggio.

E minor primary chords in comfortable inversions

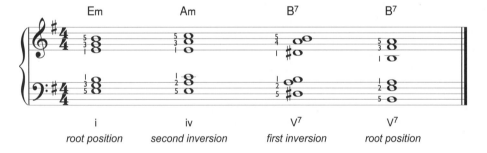

Open 5th chords in E minor

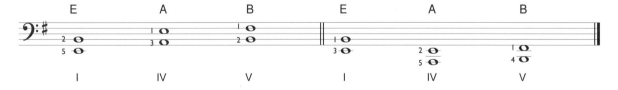

E minor scale and primary chords

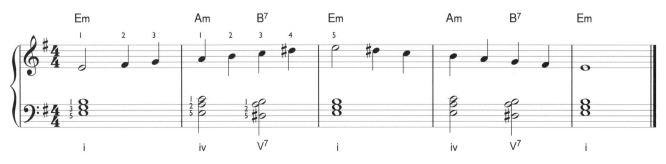

Using double thirds

Harmonise this traditional spiritual with one chord per bar, except where indicated.

- Practise the E minor scale.
- Try out the right-hand double thirds, noticing the fingering.
- Improvise using some double thirds to add variety to the original melody. An opening is suggested below.

Similar song

Tumbalalaika (begins on B)

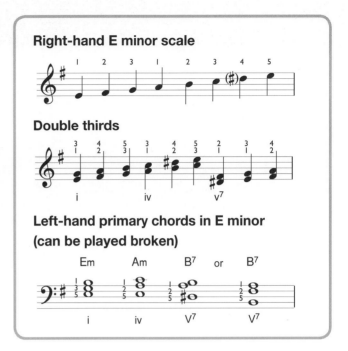

Right-hand E minor scale

Double thirds

Left-hand primary chords in E minor (can be played broken)

Go down Moses

Suggested opening for improvisation, using double thirds

etc.

Playing in D minor

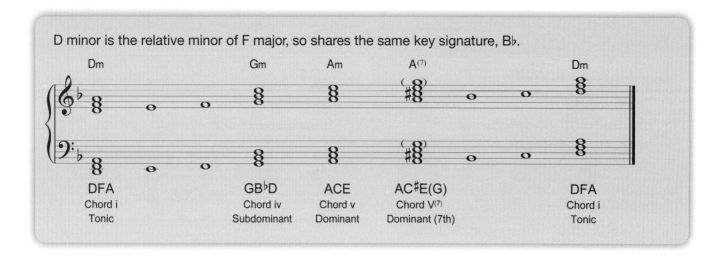

D minor is the relative minor of F major, so shares the same key signature, B♭.

A grand arpeggio progression

Play the D minor primary chords in a progression of grand arpeggios: Dm, Gm, A and Dm. Remember the C♯ accidental and use the pedal.

D minor primary chords in comfortable inversions

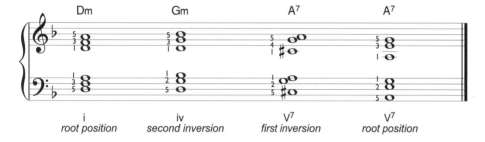

Open 5th chords in D minor

D minor scale and primary chords

- Practise the D minor scale then play and harmonise this traditional spiritual using one chord per bar.
- Continue seamlessly into an improvisation, using the same chord progression. Remember that you can invert and decorate the melody, play double thirds and repeat in different octaves. But the most important thing is to maintain a consistent left-hand chord progression.

Similar song

The Coventry carol begins on D (minor), and ends on a D major chord: this is known as a **Tierce de Picardie**.

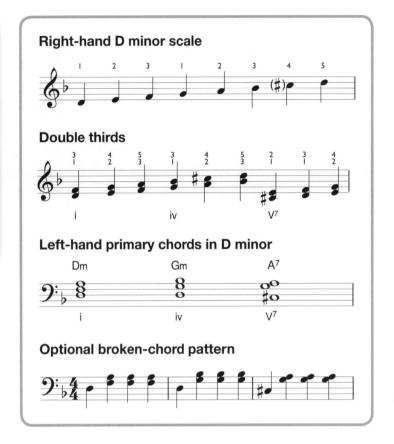

The battle of Jericho

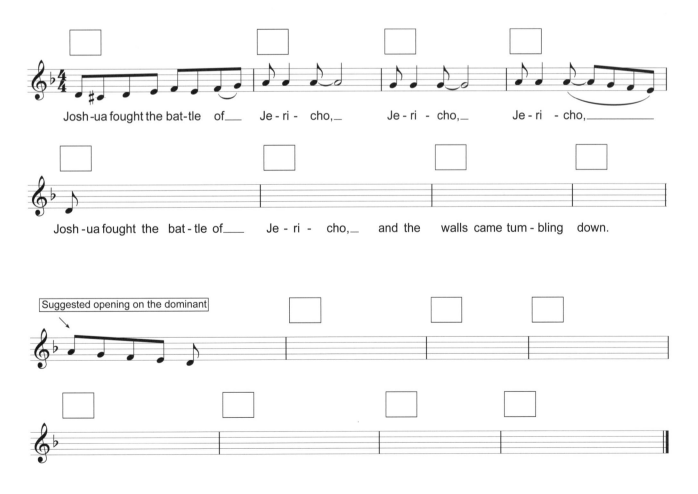

Playing in the white-note modes

The white-note modes are scales from Ancient Greece. They are wonderful to improvise with as no black notes are needed, and they each have their own delicious and distinctive sound colour. You are already familiar with the Ionian mode, as this became our major scale.

Name	White-note scale	Sound (in comparison to the major scale)	Description of the sound
Ionian	C D E F G A B C	1 2 3 4 5 6 7 8	**Major scale**
Dorian	D E F G A B C D	1 2 ♭3 4 5 6 ♭7 8	**English** English folk songs are often Dorian
Phrygian	E F G A B C D E	1 ♭2 ♭3 4 5 ♭6 ♭7 8	**Spanish** the guitar is tuned to E A D G B E
Lydian	F G A B C D E F	1 2 3 ♯4 5 6 7 8	**Spaced out** the Simpson's theme is Lydian
Mixolydian	G A B C D E F G	1 2 3 4 5 6 ♭7 8	**Gently jazzy** pop songs are often Mixolydian
Aeolian	A B C D E F G A	1 2 ♭3 4 5 ♭6 ♭7 8	**Natural minor** Celtic songs are often Aeolian

Improvisation in white-note modes (solo or group)

Try the suggested modal improvisations below and opposite. Each one uses chords and hand shapes that you are familiar with, and begins with a scale to help you hear the particular sound. They can each be played as a solo, or in groups. If playing in groups, only one person needs to play the left hand.

Using pictures to inspire improvisation

You may feel inspired by finding pictures that match the mode. For example, a postcard of the English countryside could inspire a Dorian improvisation, a photo of costumed Spanish dancers a Phrygian one, and a picture of The Simpsons could inspire a Lydian one!

Ionian (major)

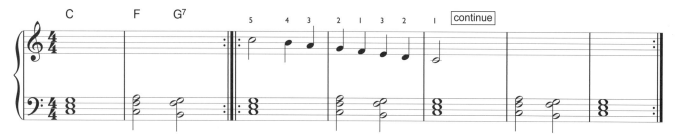

Dorian ('English')

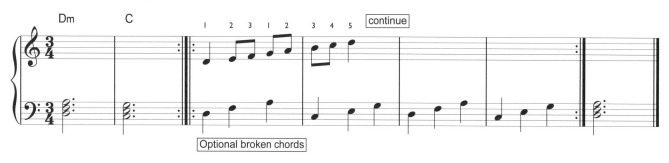

Optional broken chords

Phrygian (Spanish)

Strum like a guitar   Optional habanera rhythm   End on the key-note, E

Lydian (spaced out)

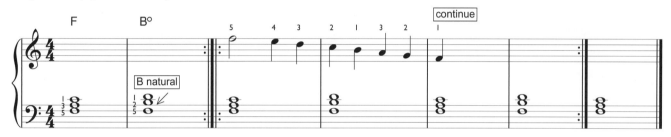

B natural

Mixolydian (gently jazzy)

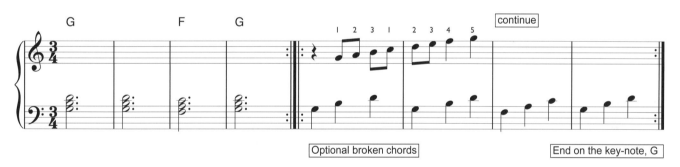

Optional broken chords   End on the key-note, G

Aeolian (natural minor)

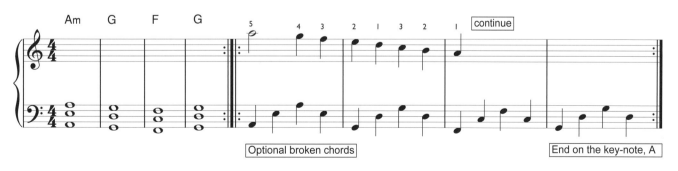

Optional broken chords   End on the key-note, A

Tip

Remember that ideas for improvisation can come from the rhythm of a song you know well, thinking in questions and answers or phrase patterns, inverting and decorating the opening melody, using double thirds and different octaves. But the most important thing is to maintain a consistent left-hand chord progression.

The Dorian mode

The Dorian mode has flattened 3rd and 7th notes compared to the major scale. It can also be thought of as having a raised 6th note compared with the natural minor (B instead of B flat in D minor). The flattened 7th is a full tone rather than a semitone below the tonic, and the chord built on the flattened 7th is always major. It is described in Roman numerals as chord ♭VII.

The drunken sailor

- First work out the chords of *Drunken sailor* while you sing or hum it. Then work out the tune and try it hands together.
- Continue seamlessly into an improvisation inspired by the song.

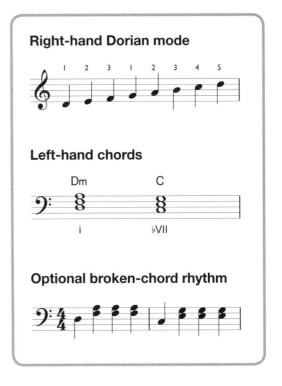

Right-hand Dorian mode

Left-hand chords

Optional broken-chord rhythm

What shall we do with the drunken sailor?

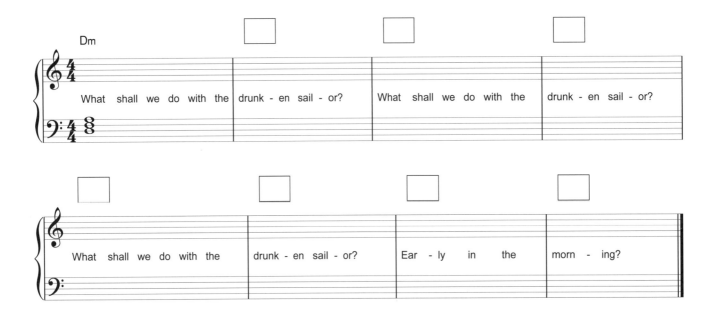

Dm

What shall we do with the | drunk - en sail - or? | What shall we do with the | drunk - en sail - or?

What shall we do with the | drunk - en sail - or? | Ear - ly in the | morn - ing?

Similar song

The ballad of Gilligan's Isle, first section
(begins on A, chords Dm and C)

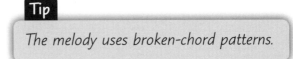

Tip

The melody uses broken-chord patterns.

More chords in the Dorian mode

Chords i (DFA), IV (GBD) and ♭VII (CEG) can be thought of as the primary chords in the Dorian mode. Notice that although chord i is minor, chord IV is major. The other chord needed in *Scarborough fair* is built on the third note of the scale, F. As F is a *minor* third from the tonic, D, and the chord is major, it is described in Roman numerals as chord ♭III.

- Work out the chords of *Scarborough fair* while you sing or hum the tune, then play it hands together.
- Improvise inspired by *Scarborough fair*. As the phrase structure is irregular (there are 19 bars!) it may be easier to create your own 16-bar improvisation to play as a chorus between verses of the song.

Scarborough fair

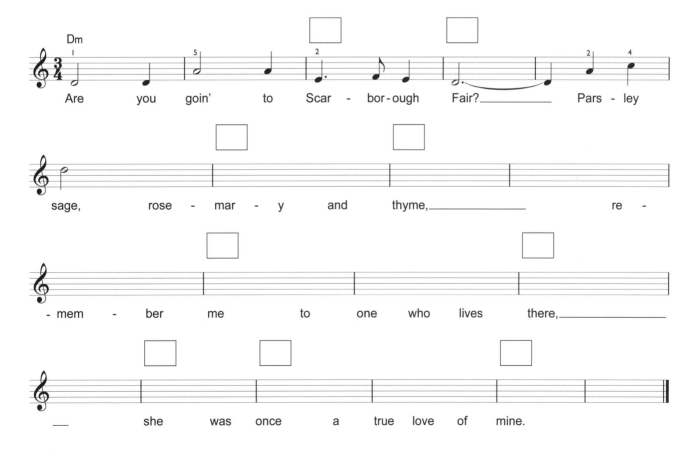

Song in the Dorian mode

Noel nouvelet (begins on D; use open 5th chords on Dm, G and A)

The Mixolydian mode

The only difference between the Mixolydian mode and our major scale is the flattened 7th note. So the chord on this note, ♭VII, and the ♭VII – I cadence are distinguishing features.

- Play the entire chord progression of *Norwegian wood* below, noticing the ♭VII – I cadence, the second section in G Dorian mode and the *da capo al fine* (repeat from the beginning to the word 'Fine').
- Then try playing the tune by ear. As you have already played the chord progression, you should be able to 'hear' the starting note in your head, and find it on the piano.
- Finally put hands together using block or broken chords.

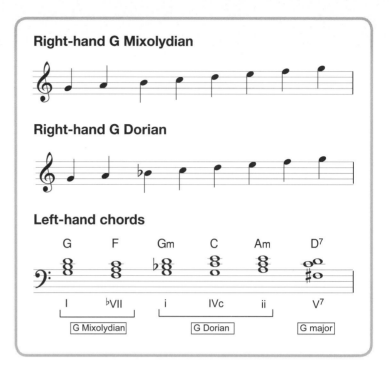

Songs in the Mixolydian mode

(chords in order of first appearance)

Flower of Scotland Roy Williamson (begins on B, chords G, D(7), C, F)

Royals Lorde (begins on D, chords G, F, C)

Norwegian wood

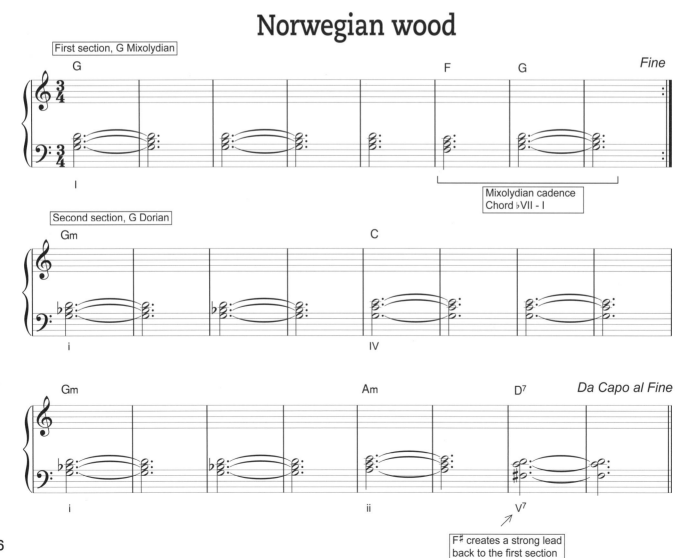

Solo or group improvising in the Aeolian mode

The Aeolian mode is the natural minor: a minor scale without the raised 7th. So chord v is always minor. Compared to the major scale it has a flattened 3rd, 6th and 7th, so the chord on the 6th note of the scale is known as chord ♭VI.

To play solo

- Choose one left-hand repeated bass and one right-hand position and improvise in the usual way.
- Remember to set a steady (3-time) pulse and play four left-hand bars as an introduction.
- Bring your improvisation to an end on the key-note and chord (A minor).

To play with two or more people

- The leader must play a **left-hand repeated bass**. Everyone else can choose whether to play with one or both hands.
- The leader sets a steady pulse and guides left-hand players to enter at two-bar intervals. Then right-hand players enter, listening and responding to each other.
- Players can bring their own parts to an end individually, or be guided to a close on the key-note and chord (A minor).

Variations: feel free to play your own rhythmic variations, adapt the basses to improvise in 4-time and transpose to any Aeolian (natural minor) key.

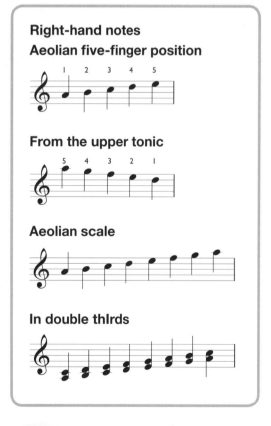

Tip

Maintain a strong sense of pulse, consistent left hand, and play what you feel like playing! Don't think too hard!

The original piano accompaniment is intrinsic to this song, but does not include the melody. The suggested introduction and broken-chord accompaniment aim to convey the composers' ideas as simply and effectively as possible, as well as allowing the right hand to play the melody.

- Work out the chords first.
- Choose whether to play them in the style of the introduction, while you sing or hum the tune, or play the right-hand tune and left-hand accompaniment, as outlined.

Songs and themes in the Aeolian mode

(chords in order of appearance)

The banquet from *Amélie* (chords Am and Em)
Love song The Cure (chords Am, G, F, Em, C)
Wonderwall Oasis (chords Am, C, G, Dm, F)

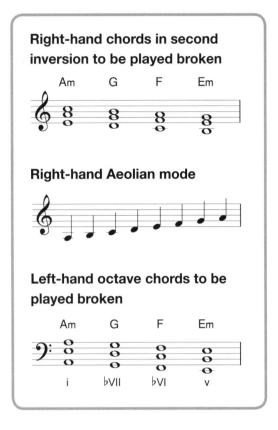

Right-hand chords in second inversion to be played broken

Right-hand Aeolian mode

Left-hand octave chords to be played broken

The power of love

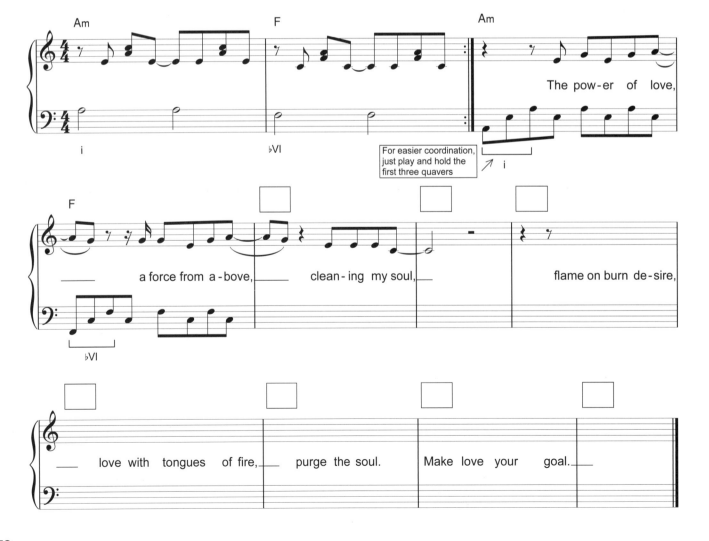

Introducing secondary chords in C major

There is a chord for every note of the scale. You know the primary chords: chords I (tonic), IV (subdominant) and V⁽⁷⁾ (dominant ⁽⁷⁾). The **secondary chords** are chords ii (**supertonic**), iii (**mediant**) and vi (**submediant**). Chord vii (leading note) is a **diminished chord**. Diminished chords have a minor third and a flattened or 'diminished' fifth.

A broken-chord progression

Create your own broken-chord (or grand arpeggio) progression with four different chords, ending on the tonic. For example:

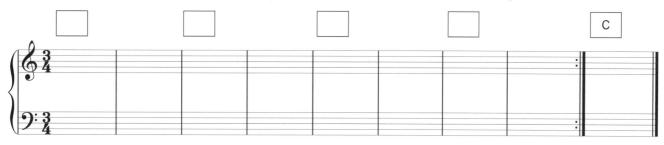

Fill in the boxes below with your chosen chord symbols, and then improvise, playing broken chords ascending, or descending, over as many octaves as you choose. Use the pedal.

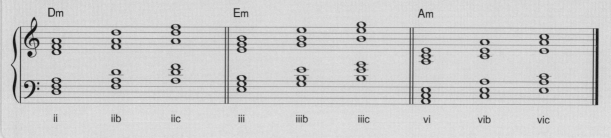

Inversions

Chords can be inverted for ease of movement and to express different musical qualities. Root position chords sound grounded, first inversions have a sense of being on the move and second inversions can feel suspended in mid-air. The lower case 'b' and 'c' indicate first and second inversions respectively.

Try playing the theme from *Chariots of Fire* Vangelis (begins on C, with chords F, C, Em, Dm)
Or *Skaters' Waltz* (begins on E, chords C, Dm, Em, Am, G⁷)

The 1950s chord progression

As the name suggests, the chord progression **I vi IV V** became very popular in the 1950s.

- Practise the progression, then play it while you sing or hum the tune *Heart and soul*.
- Then work out the tune to play with left-hand chords.
- Finally, improvise over the progression with either the C major or C pentatonic scale.

Similar songs

Dream, dream, dream Everly Brothers (begins on E)

The way you look tonight Jerome Kern (begins on G)

We go together (begins on E) from *Grease*

Right-hand C major

Right-hand C pentatonic with optional E flat

Best five-finger position for improvising

Left-hand chords for right-hand tune

Fun broken chords to accompany singing

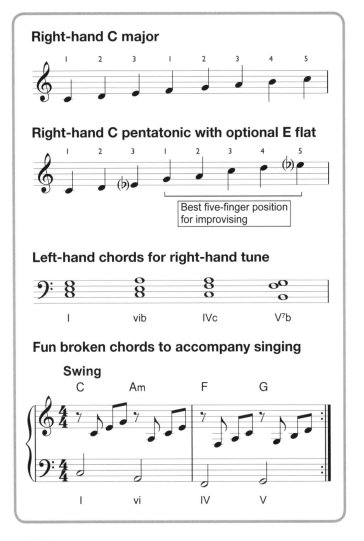

Tip

Songs with the 1950s and doo-wop chord progressions can be sung simultaneously!

Heart and soul

Play at this pitch, or an octave lower

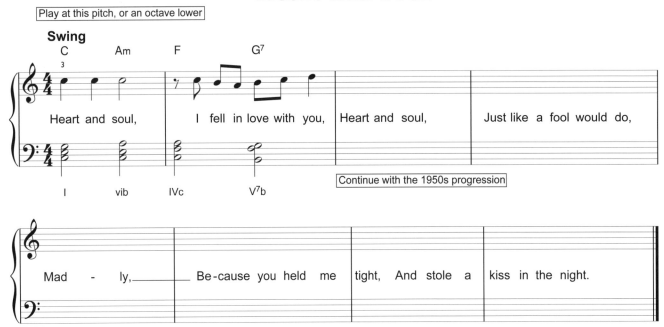

Continue with the 1950s progression

The doo-wop progression

The **doo-wop progression: I vi ii V** developed in the 1950s with the substitution of chord ii for chord IV.

Notice also the **jazz scale**, created from the major and ♭3 pentatonic scales with an added ♭7.

- Sing *Santa baby* while you play the chords.
- Then work out the tune to play with the left-hand chords.
- Finally, improvise over the doo-wop progression with either C major or the C jazz scale.

Right-hand C major

Right-hand C jazz scale

Left-hand chords

Fun and easy chords to accompany singing

Similar songs

Blue moon (begins on G)
Sleigh ride chorus (begins on G)

Tip *The 1950s and doo-wop progressions are easy to transpose for more comfortable singing.*

Santa baby

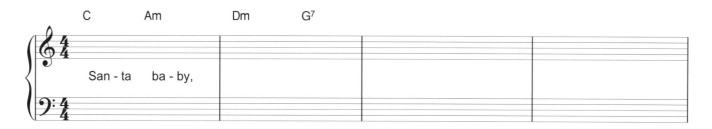

San - ta   ba - by,

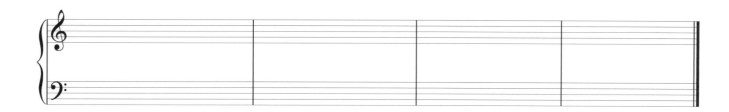

Solo or group improvising in C major

To play solo

- Choose one left-hand repeated bass and one right-hand position and improvise in the usual way.
- Remember to set a steady pulse and play four left-hand bars as an introduction.
- Bring your improvisation to an end on the key-note and chord (C major).

To play with two or more people

- The leader must play a left-hand repeated bass. Everyone else can choose whether to play with one or both hands.

- The leader sets a steady pulse and guides left-hand players to enter at two-bar intervals. Then right-hand players enter, listening and responding to each other.
- Players can bring their own parts to an end individually, or be guided to a close on the key-note and chord.

Variations

- Left-hand ideas can be played with rhythmic variations within the chord structure, and the whole improvisation can be transposed to any major key.

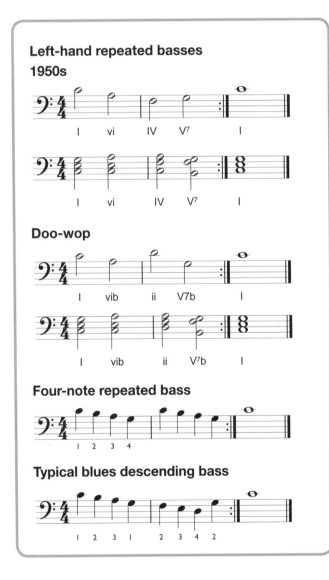

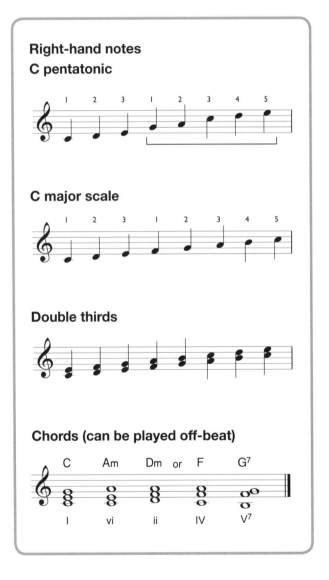

The four-chord trick

Many songs can be harmonised by simply adding chord vi to the three primary chords.

- Sing or play *Let's twist again* while you work out the chords, then put hands together.
- Notice that the tune is pentatonic, using both the root and inverted hand positions. This makes it particularly easy to slip seamlessly into an improvisation.
- You could also use the walking-bass style to accompany singing.

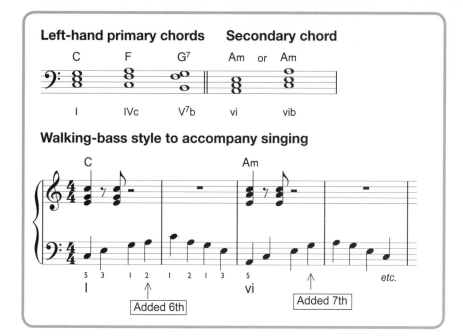

Similar songs

Dance with me tonight Olly Murs (begins on C, chords C, Am, F, G)

Lego house Ed Sheeran (begins on G, chords C, G, Am, F)

Truly madly deeply Savage Garden (begins on C, chords C, G, F, chorus Am, G, F, G)

Let's twist again

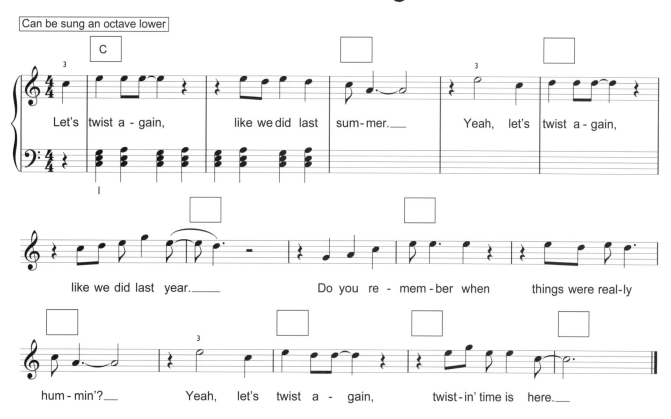

Secondary chord substitutions

Secondary chords can substitute primary chords. They tend to replace those that include two of the same notes. So, in C major, chord I (CEG) can be substituted by chord iii (EGB) or vi (ACE).

Chord IV (FAC) can be substituted by chord ii (DFA) or vi (ACE).

Chord V^7 (GBDF) can be substituted by chord ii (DFA) or iii (EGB).

- Play the primary chord progression while you sing, hum or play the tune.
- Then play the bracketed secondary chord substitutions. Notice that the doo-wop progression (I vi ii V) arises naturally out of the substitutions!
- Finally improvise over the secondary-chord progression.

Left-hand primary chords			Secondary chords	
C	F	G^7	Dm	Am
I	IVc	V^7b	ii	vi

He's got the whole world

Similar songs to try secondary chord substitutions

Mary had a little lamb: play the usual progression: C, C, $G^{(7)}$, C, then try C, Am, $G^{(7)}$, C.
Old Macdonald: play the usual progression: C, C, F, C, C, $G^{(7)}$, C, then try C, Em, F, C, Dm, $G^{(7)}$ C.
Try adding one or two secondary chords to any progression you know well.

Harmonic rhythm

This is the rate at which chords change. Notice that *Danny boy* begins with one chord per bar, then has two chords per bar, and the penultimate bar has three chords. Notice, also, that the secondary chords appear with the increasing harmonic rhythm, and combine to add intensity and convey the rising passion of this love song.

- Play the chords in both hands while you sing or hum the tune.
- When confident, try accompanying *Danny boy* with the suggested broken-chord rhythm.
- Then try playing the right-hand tune with left-hand chords, blocked or broken.

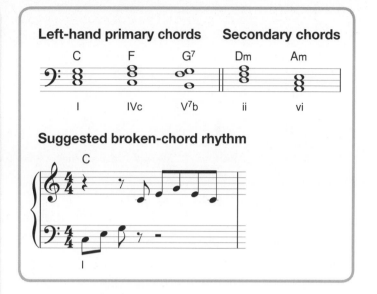

Similar songs (chords in order of first appearance)

Fields of gold Sting (chords Am, F, G, C)
Thinking out loud Ed Sheeran (C, F, G, Dm, Am)
Wonderful tonight Eric Clapton (C, G$^{(7)}$, F, Am, Dm)
Everything I do, I do it for you Bryan Adams (C, G, F, Dm)

Danny boy

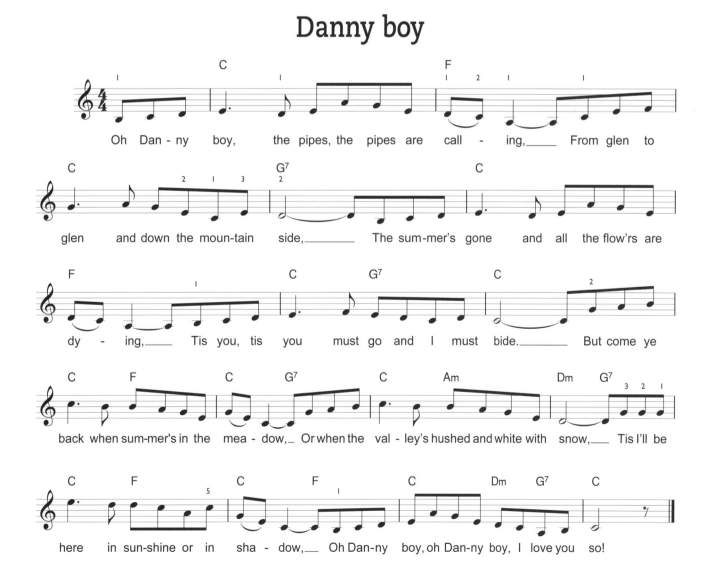

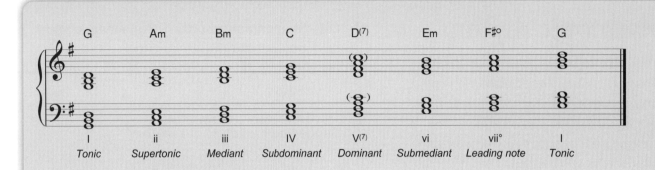

G	Am	Bm	C	D(7)	Em	F#°	G
I	ii	iii	IV	V(7)	vi	vii°	I
Tonic	Supertonic	Mediant	Subdominant	Dominant	Submediant	Leading note	Tonic

- Sing, hum or play *God save the Queen* with the primary chords given.
- Then follow the bracketed chord symbols to hear the added colour that comes with the use of secondary chords.
- Notice that the doo-wop progression (I vi ii V) arises naturally out of the substitutions on the second and third lines, with a quick change of chord to arrive back 'home' on time!

Left-hand chords

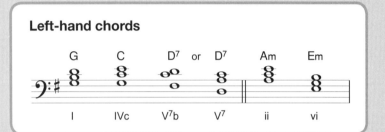

G	C	D⁷ or D⁷	Am	Em
I	IVc	V⁷b V⁷	ii	vi

God save the Queen

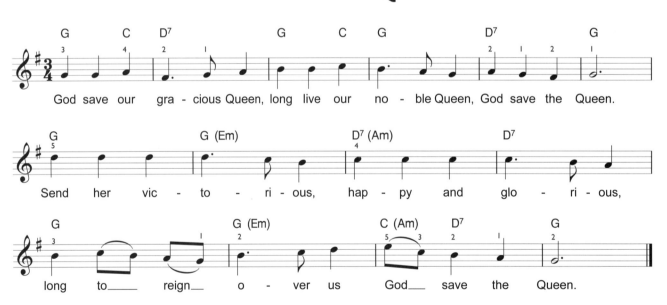

God save our gra - cious Queen, long live our no - ble Queen, God save the Queen.

Send her vic - to - ri - ous, hap - py and glo - ri - ous,

long to reign o - ver us God save the Queen.

Similar songs (chords in order of first appearance)

The red flag (chords G, D(7), Am, Em)

True colours Phil Collins/Cyndi Lauper (chorus C, G, D(7), Em)

Take me home country roads John Denver (chords G, Em, D(7), C)

- First, sing or hum the tune while you work out the progression in block chords (one chord per bar except where indicated).
- Then work out the right-hand tune and play hands together.
- You can also improvise over the chord progression.

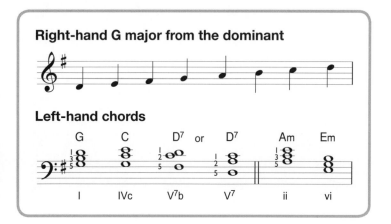

Right-hand G major from the dominant

Left-hand chords

Away in a manger

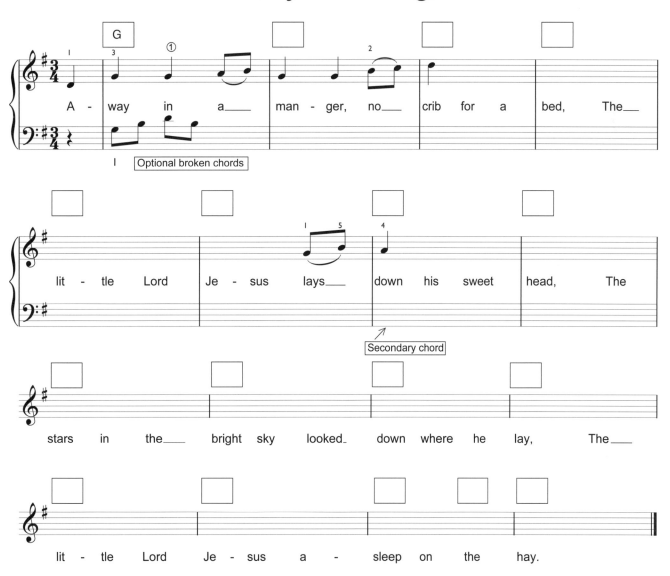

A - way in a___ man - ger, no___ crib for a bed, The___

Optional broken chords

lit - tle Lord Je - sus lays___ down his sweet head, The

Secondary chord

stars in the___ bright sky looked_ down where he lay, The___

lit - tle Lord Je - sus a - sleep on the hay.

Similar songs (chords in order of first appearance)

The ashgrove (first section) (chords G, Em, Am, D(7), C)

She's the one Robbie Williams (chords, G, C, Am, D(7))

Every breath you take (first section) Sting (chords G, Em, C, D(7))

Let her go Passenger (chords D, C, G, Em, Bm)

Introducing secondary chords in F major

Notice that the seventh has been added to chord ii as an option. All chords can have an added seventh, or any other added note. They are indicated by a superscript number in the chord symbol, such as ii^7 or F^6.

F	$Gm^{(7)}$	Am	B♭	$C^{(7)}$	Dm	E°	F
I	$ii^{(7)}$	iii	IV	$V^{(7)}$	vi	vii°	I
Tonic	Supertonic	Mediant	Subdominant	Dominant	Submediant	Leading note	Tonic

- First work out the chords and tune for *Stranger in paradise* and put hands together.
- Then continue seamlessly into an improvisation over the three-chord progression.

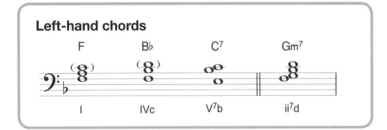

Left-hand chords

F	B♭	C^7	Gm^7
I	IVc	V^7b	ii^7d

Similar songs

The first man you remember from *Aspects of Love* (chords $Gm^{(7)}$, $C^{(7)}$, F)

Love is all around Wet, Wet, Wet (chords F, $Gm^{(7)}$, $C^{(7)}$, F, B♭)

Stranger in paradise from *Kismet*

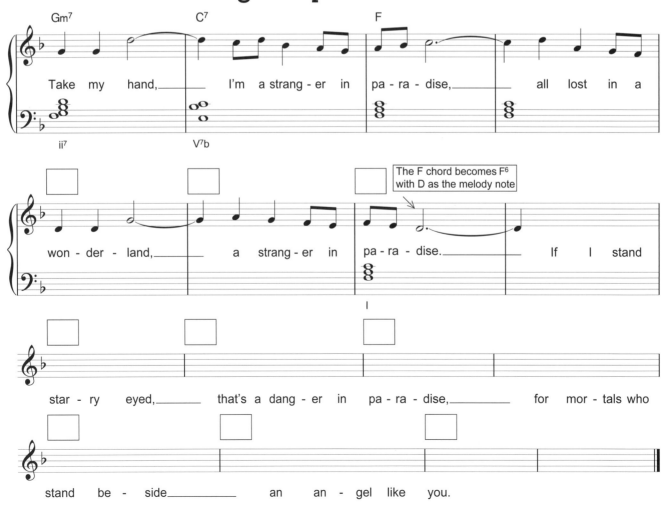

Take my hand, I'm a strang - er in pa - ra - dise, all lost in a

won - der - land, a strang - er in pa - ra - dise. If I stand

star - ry eyed, that's a dang - er in pa - ra - dise, for mor - tals who

stand be - side an an - gel like you.

The F chord becomes F^6 with D as the melody note

- Play *Wild mountain thyme*, completing the chord progression.
- Then improvise over the progression using F pentatonic.

Similar songs (chords in order of first appearance)

The scientist Coldplay (chords Dm, B♭, F, C)
Wings Birdy (chords F, Am, B♭, Dm, C)
Price tag Jessie J (chords F, Am, Dm, B♭)
Honey, honey from *Mamma Mia* (chords F, B♭, Dm, C(7))
Pretty Woman (chords F, Dm, B♭, C(7))

Tip

When the left-hand chord progression needs concentration just use a right-hand five-finger position to improvise. You can change octaves for variety.

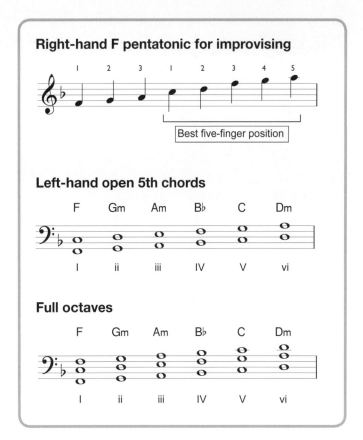

Wild mountain thyme

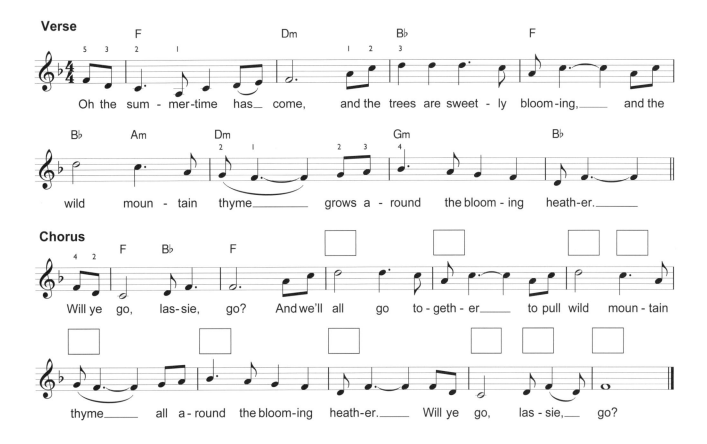

Bass lines

Many bass lines ascend or descend in recognisable patterns (*Pachelbel's canon*) or by step (*Streets of London*). A bass line is created through the choice of root position or inverted chords. Notice that inverted chords can be indicated with letter names: C/E means a C major chord with E as the lowest note (first inversion).

- Play each of the left-hand progression from *Pachelbel's canon* below.
- Then choose your favourite as a bass for improvisation. You can use the F major scale, double thirds or chords in your right hand.

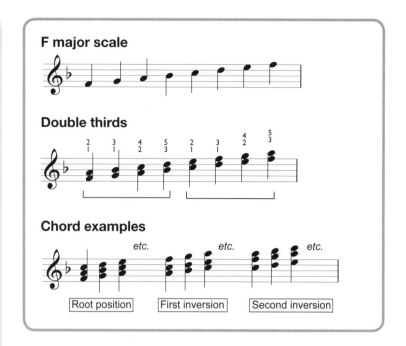

F major scale

Double thirds

Chord examples

Root position | First inversion | Second inversion

Similar songs (chords in order of first appearance)

You're beautiful James Blunt (chords F, C/E, Dm, B♭)

My heart will go on from *Titanic* (chords F, C/E, B♭/D, C, Dm, Am, Gm)

Let it be The Beatles (chords F, C/E, Dm, B♭)

Pachelbel's chord progression

Left-hand single bass notes

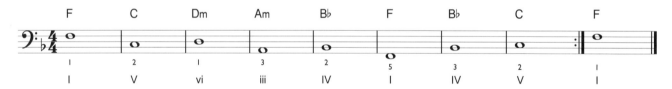

Left-hand root position chords (can be played broken)

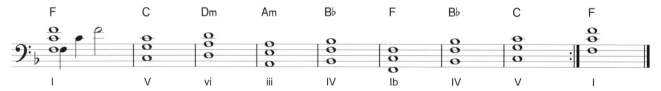

Left-hand chords with inversions to create a bassline that ascends and descends by step

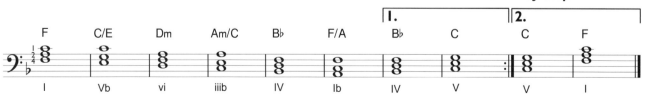

This progression is used in the first and last sections of *Streets of London*.

Pub-style accompaniments

Pub (or knees-up) style accompaniments are characterised by a 'boom ching' rhythm between left and right hands.

- Work out the progression with one block chord per bar, while you sing or hum the tune.
- Then try the pub-style accompaniment shown.

Similar songs

(chords in order of first appearance)

Knees up Mother Brown
  (chords C, F, G)
You are my sunshine
  (chords C, F, G)

Step in time from *Mary Poppins*

You can also try playing the pub-style accompaniment in the left hand and the melody in the right hand:

Chord ♭VII in a major key

You have been introduced to chord ♭VII in the Dorian, Mixolydian and Aeolian (natural minor) modes. It is also frequently used in major keys for a funky, laid-back effect.

- Choose a song and play the chord progression with both hands while you sing or hum the tune.
- Then work out the right-hand tune for the left-hand chords.
- You can also improvise over part or all of the progression using the right-hand pentatonic or major scale.

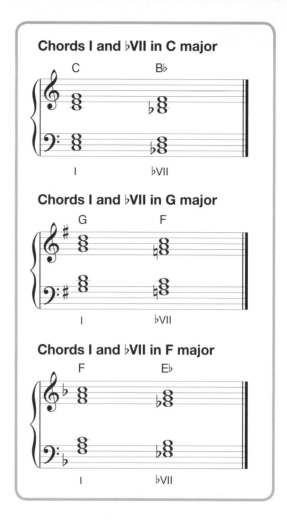

Angels

Robbie Williams (in C major)

(verse begins on low G in the middle of the second bar, chorus begins on C)

Verse

```
C / / /   C / / /
C / / /   C / / /   F / / /   G / / /
C / / /   C / / /   F / / /   G / / /
Dm / / /  F / / /   Am / / /  F / / /
```

Chorus

```
B♭ / / /  Am/ / /   C / / /   B♭ / Am /
C / / /   G / / /   Am / / /  F / / /
C / / /   G / / /   Am / / /  F / / /
C / / /   Dm / / /  B♭ / F / C / / /
```

I'm a believer from *Shrek*

The Monkees (in F major)

(verse and chorus begin on F)

Verse

```
F / / /   C⁷ / / /  F / / /   F / / /
F / / /   C⁷ / / /  F / / /   F / / /
B♭ / / /  F / / /   B♭ / / /  F / / /
B♭ / / /  F / / /   C⁷ / / /  C⁷ / / /
```

Chorus

```
F / B♭ /  F / B♭ /  F / B♭ /  F / B♭ /
F / B♭ /  F / B♭ /  F / B♭ /  F / B♭ /
F / / /   B♭ / / /  F / / /   E♭ / / /
C⁷ / / /  C / / /
```

I'll be there for you

from *Friends* The Rembrandts (in G major)

(verse begins on low D, chorus on high D)

Verse

```
G / / /   G / / /   G / / /   F / / /
G / / /   G / / /   G / / /   Bm / / /
F / / /   Am / / /  G / / /   G / / /
F / / /   C / / /   D / / /   D / / /
```

Chorus

```
G / / /   C / / /   D / / /   D / / /
G / / /   C / / /   D / / /   D / / /
G / / /   C / / /   D / / /   D / / /
F / / /   F / / /
```

Similar songs

(chords in order of first appearance)

Music of the night (first section) from *Phantom of the opera* (C major; chords C, G⁽⁷⁾, F, B♭)

I can see clearly now Johnny Nash (G major; chords G, C, D⁽⁷⁾, F)

All my loving The Beatles (F major; chords Gm, C⁽⁷⁾, F, Dm, B♭, E♭ and D♭⁺ (D♭ F A)

Secondary dominants

G$^{(7)}$, C$^{(7)}$ and D$^{(7)}$ are dominants in the keys of C, F and G major respectively. When dominant (sevenths) like these appear in keys where they are not the dominant, they are called **secondary dominants**. So C$^{(7)}$ and D$^{(7)}$ are secondary dominants in the key of C. Play these two progressions to hear and understand secondary dominants:

Primary chord progression:

With secondary dominant substitutions:

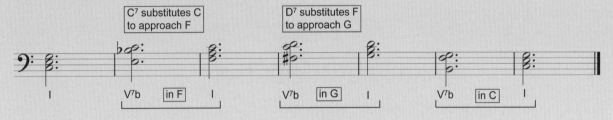

Now play the chord progression below while you sing or hum *Amazing grace*. Then play it with the secondary dominant substitutions to hear the added colour and intensity.

Amazing grace

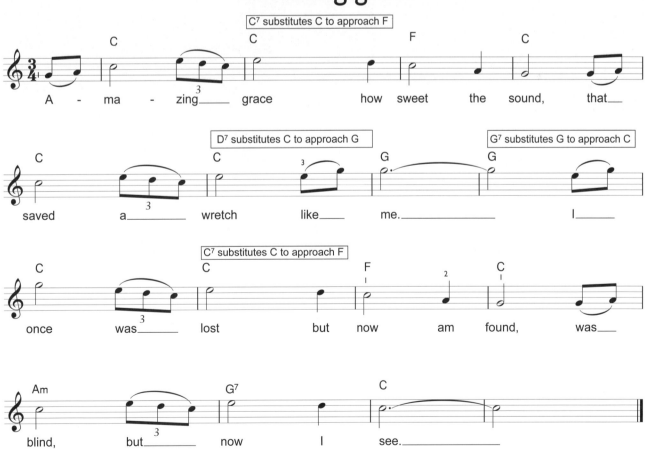

Similar songs to try with secondary dominants

Mary had a little lamb play the usual progression C, C, G$^{(7)}$, C, then try C, D$^{(7)}$, G$^{(7)}$, C

Old Macdonald play the usual progression C, C, F, C, C, G$^{(7)}$, C then try C, C$^{(7)}$, F, C, D$^{(7)}$, G$^{(7)}$, C

Chromatic passing notes

You have played **diatonic passing notes** (notes which are included in the scale but not the accompanying chord). **Chromatic passing notes** are not included in either the scale or the current chord. They are usually approached and left by semitone.

- Work out the progression in block chords while you sing or hum the tune.
- Then complete the right-hand tune, with its chromatic passing notes, using occasional right-hand chords as shown, and try it hands together.
- Remember that you can always choose just to play the chords to accompany singing (see page 91).

Similar songs (chords in order of first appearance)

Supercalifragilisticexpialidocious from *Mary Poppins* (chords C, G⁽⁷⁾, Dm, F)

So long, farewell from *The sound of music* (chords C, G⁽⁷⁾)

Libiamo (The drinking song) first section from *La Traviata*, Verdi (chords C, G⁽⁷⁾, F)

Roll out the barrel

I'd do anything from *Oliver*

Similar songs (chords in order of first appearance; try using inversions)

Someone like you Adele (chords C, Em/B, Am, F, G, Dm)

Somewhere only we know Keane/Lily Allen (chords C, Em/B, Dm, G, Am, Em, F, G⁷)

Secondary dominant sequences

This classic and beautiful progression rises through dominant – tonic sequences in the subdominant, dominant and relative minor. Play it as written, enjoying the wonderful sound.

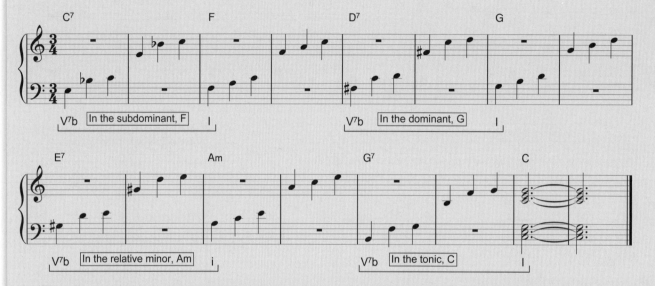

- Play the chord progression below while you sing or hum *Do-re-mi* from *The sound of music*. Notice the same rising secondary dominant sequence in the second half, bringing a great sense of joy to the song.

Do-re-mi

Similar songs and themes

(chords in order of first appearance)

La Donna e Mobile from *Rigoletto* Verdi (begins on E, chords C, G⁽⁷⁾, D⁽⁷⁾-G, E⁽⁷⁾-Am)

Barcarolle from *The Tales of Hoffman*, by Offenbach (begins on E, chords C, G⁷, C⁷-F, D⁷-G, C⁰)

Hallelujah Leonard Cohen (begins on E, chords C, Am, F, G, E⁷-Am)

Tip

Try transposing the sequence into G and F major. You will find it very useful for other songs.

Modulations

Modulations are usually established with perfect cadences in the new key. The most usual modulation in a major key is to the dominant.

- Play the chords, while you sing or hum the tune, noticing the modulations. Then play the right-hand tune with left-hand chords.

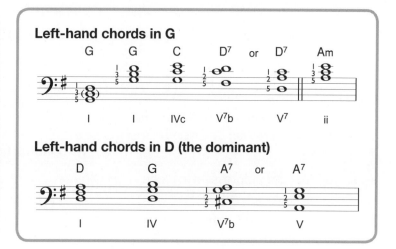

The star-spangled banner

Similar songs (chords in order of first appearance)

Just give me a reason Pink (chords G, C, Em, A$^{(7)}$, D, D$^{(7)}$, Bm, Am)

The Archers theme (chords G, C, Em, A$^{(7)}$, D, Am, D$^{(7)}$)

Secondary dominants don't always resolve onto their tonics: the B major chord in this song doesn't resolve onto its tonic, E minor. Instead it can be thought of as majoring chord iii (iii#3), which brings a feeling of strength and hope.

- Work out the progression in block chords while you sing or hum the tune.
- Then work out the right-hand tune, and try it hands together.

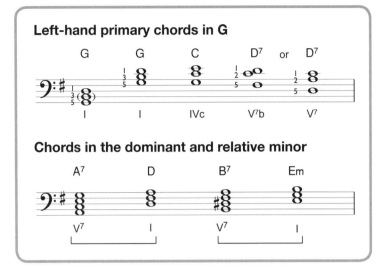

It's a long way to Tipperary

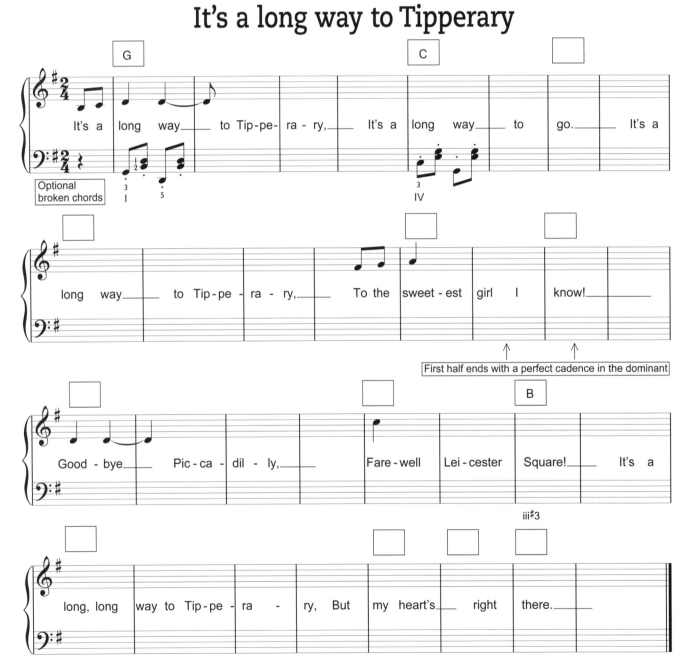

Similar songs (chords in order of first appearance)

Yesterday The Beatles (chords G, B[7], Em, C, D, A[7], D[7])

Pack up your troubles in your old kit bag (chords G, B[7], Em, C, A[7], D, D[7], G[7])

- Work out the progression in block chords then complete the right-hand tune, and try it hands together.

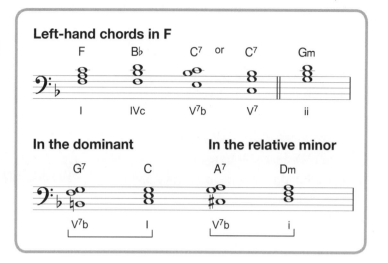

Similar songs

(chords in order of first appearance)

While shepherds watched their flocks (begins on low C, chords F, B♭, G⁽⁷⁾-C)

Streets of London Ralph McTell (chords F, C/E, Dm, Am/C, B♭, F/A, C, Am, G⁽⁷⁾-C)

We wish you a merry Christmas

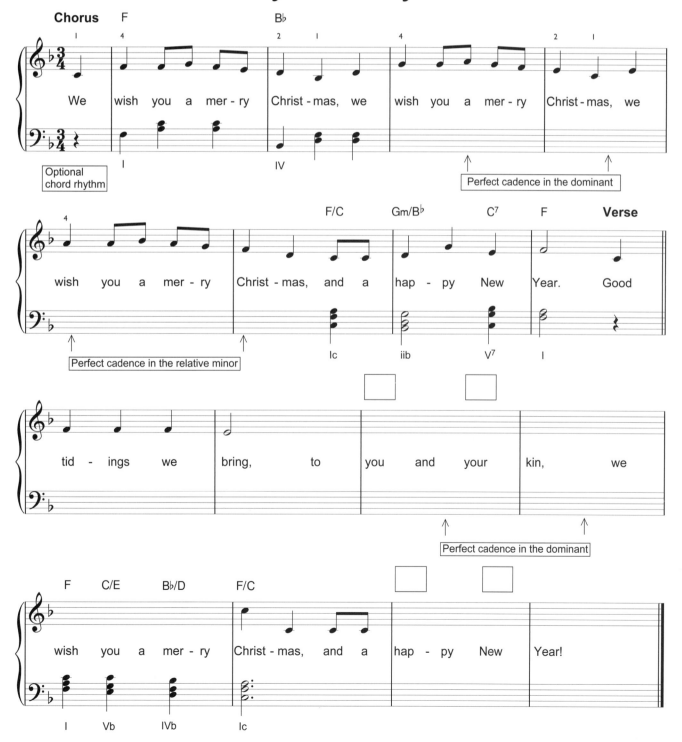

Flattening the third of a major chord to make it minor creates a beautiful effect filled with longing. In *O sole mio* Chord IV (B♭, D, F) is made minor: IV♭3 (B♭, D♭, F).

- Work out the chords while you sing or hum the tune.
- Complete the tune, aiming to play it in double thirds and chords. Then accompany it with the habanera rhythm.

Left-hand chords in habanera rhythm

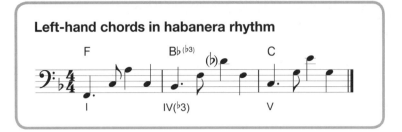

Similar songs (chords in order of first appearance)

Hello goodbye The Beatles (chords Gm, F, C⁽⁷⁾, Dm, B♭, B♭m)

How deep is your love? The Bee Gees (chords F, C⁽⁷⁾, B♭, D⁽⁷⁾, Gm, B♭m)

Jar of hearts chorus Christina Perri (chords F, C, Dm, B♭, B♭m)

O sole mio

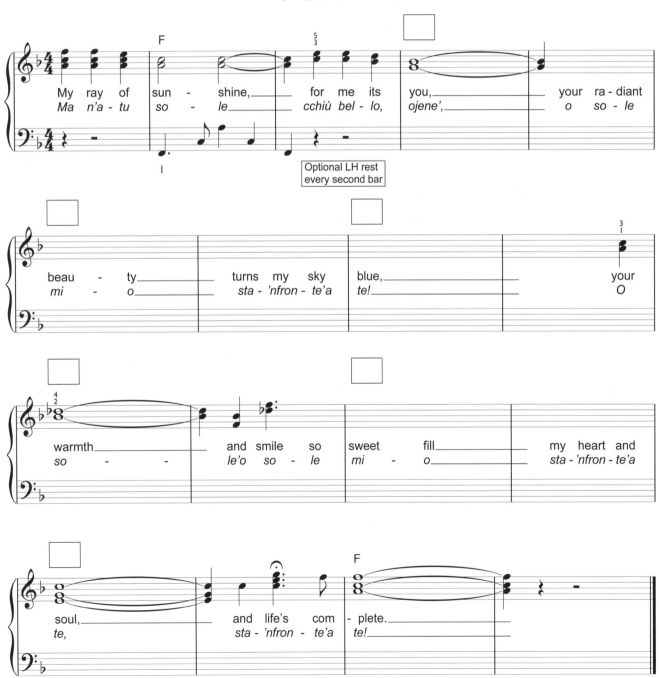

Optional LH rest every second bar

Aura Lea is an American folk song made popular by Elvis Presley's harmonisation in *Love me tender*.

- Complete the first harmonisation with primary chords, following the horizontal arrows.
- Follow the dashed arrows to create an Elvis-style harmonisation, completing the remaining empty boxes with secondary dominant (major) chords to create the V^7-I progressions shown opposite.

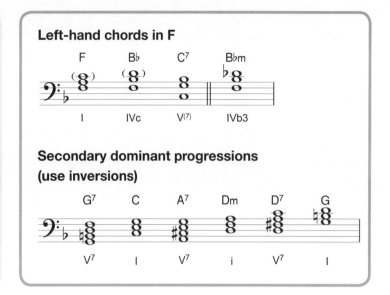

Left-hand chords in F

Secondary dominant progressions (use inversions)

Aura lea

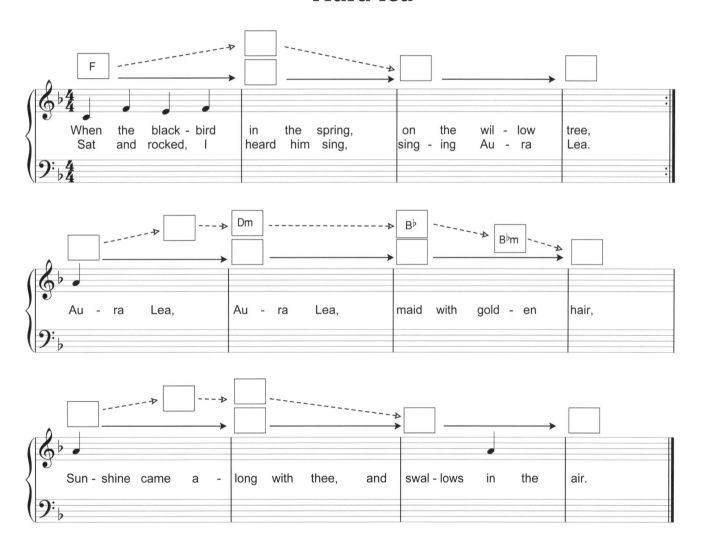

Similar songs (chords in order of first appearance)

Don't dilly dally (my old man) (chords F, $G^{(7)}$-$C^{(7)}$, $A^{(7)}$-Dm, $Gm^{(7)}$)

Congratulations Cliff Richard (chords F, $G^{(7)}$-$C^{(7)}$, $D^{(7)}$-Gm)

Maybe it's because I'm a Londoner (chords F, $D^{(7)}$-$G^{(7)}$-$C^{(7)}$ $A^{(7)}$-$D^{(7)}$-Gm)

Introducing secondary chords in A minor

Notice the similarity between the chords in A minor and its relative major, C major. The only difference is due to the optional raised 7th note, G♯. The 6th note of the scale may also be raised in minor keys, usually as part of the melody rather than the harmony. So, in A minor, F may become F♯.

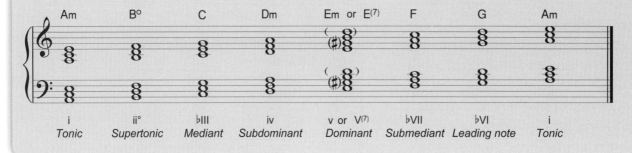

i	ii°	♭III	iv	v or V⁽⁷⁾	♭VII	♭VI	i
Tonic	Supertonic	Mediant	Subdominant	Dominant	Submediant	Leading note	Tonic

The circle of fifths

The circle of fifths is a chord progression, which descends a fifth and ascends a fourth through an octave.

- First play the left hand. It can be played in two separate eight-bar, or one continuous sixteen-bar sequence.
- Then improvise with your right hand. You may find yourself using descending sequences to mirror the left-hand progression.

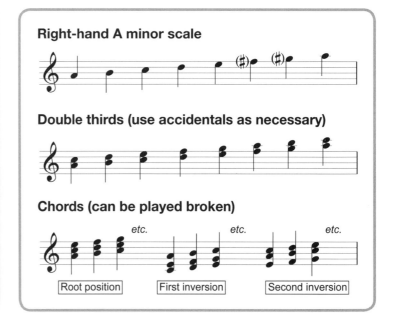

Right-hand A minor scale

Double thirds (use accidentals as necessary)

Chords (can be played broken)

Root position   First inversion   Second inversion

This chord progression is used in *Fly me to the moon*. See page 111 for the complete chords.

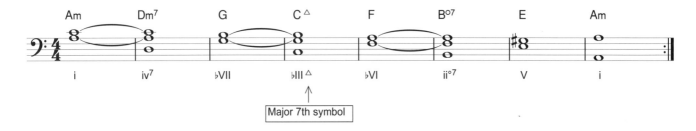

Major 7th symbol

This chord progression is used in *Autumn leaves*. The tune begins on an A with a three-note upbeat and the chords need to be played an octave higher. The song continues with chords E⁷, Am, G⁷, C, Dm.

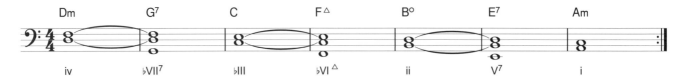

It is very easy to slip in and out of the relative major because no additional sharps or flats are required: chords ♭III and ♭VII in the minor are the tonic and dominant in the relative major.

- Play the left-hand waltz-style chords, noticing the brief modulation to C major.
- Then work out the tune (you'll need the odd chromatic note) and try it hands together.
- Finally, improvise over the chord progression.

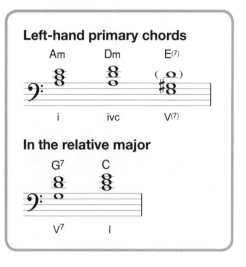

Left-hand primary chords

In the relative major

Anniversary song from *The waves of the Danube*

Introducing secondary chords in E minor

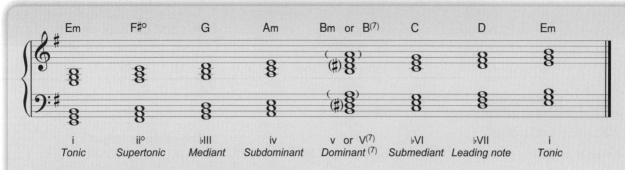

Em	F#°	G	Am	Bm or B(7)	C	D	Em
i	ii°	♭III	iv	v or V(7)	♭VI	♭VII	i
Tonic	Supertonic	Mediant	Subdominant	Dominant (7)	Submediant	Leading note	Tonic

- Work out the chords while you sing or hum *We three kings*.
- Then work out the right-hand tune and put hands together.
- Notice that the chorus is in the relative, G major.

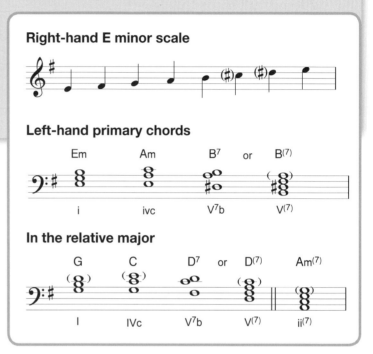

Right-hand E minor scale

Left-hand primary chords

Em	Am	B⁷ or B(7)
i	ivc	V⁷b V(7)

In the relative major

G	C	D⁷ or D(7)	Am(7)
I	IVc	V⁷b V(7)	ii(7)

Similar songs

(chords in order of first appearance)

The Sound of Silence Simon and Garfunkel
(chords Em, D, C, G)

Kalinka (chorus in Em, chords B⁷, Em, verse in G major, chords G, D⁷, C)

All of me John Legend (verse in E minor, chords Em, C, G, D, Am, chorus in G major, chords G, Em, C, D⁷)

We three kings

Verse

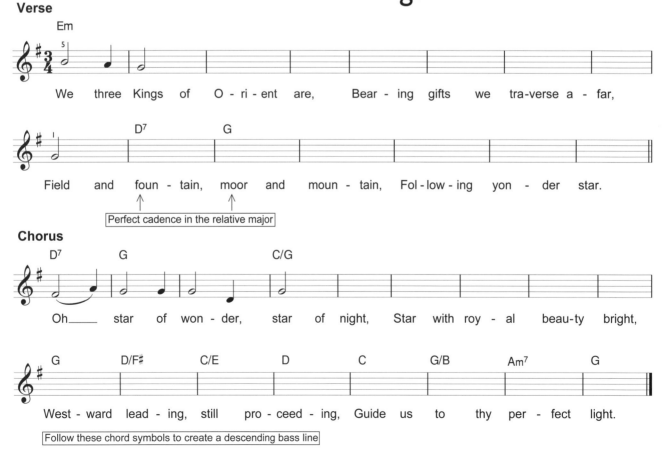

Em

We three Kings of O - ri - ent are, Bear - ing gifts we tra-verse a - far,

D⁷   G

Field and foun - tain, moor and moun - tain, Fol - low - ing yon - der star.

↑   ↑
Perfect cadence in the relative major

Chorus

D⁷   G   C/G

Oh___ star of won - der, star of night, Star with roy - al beau-ty bright,

G   D/F#   C/E   D   C   G/B   Am⁷   G

West - ward lead - ing, still pro - ceed - ing, Guide us to thy per - fect light.

Follow these chord symbols to create a descending bass line

104

Chromatic notes in the bass line sound very poignant. The chromatic bass note in this song, C♯, turns the minor chord iv (A,C,E) into a major chord: A,C♯,E.

- Work out the chords while you sing or hum the tune, then invert them to fit the descending bass line. Notice the useful left-hand Ic-V progression.
- Then work out the right-hand tune, and try hands together.
- Finally, improvise.

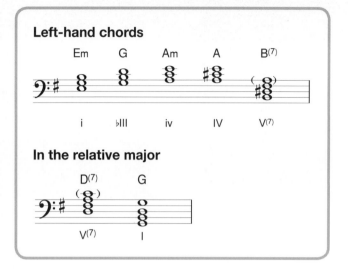

Left-hand chords

In the relative major

House of the Rising Sun

There is a house in New Or - leans, They call the Ris - ing Sun, And it's been the ruin of ma - ny a poor boy, And me I know I'm one.

Find the right chords to use this descending bass line

Perfect cadence in the relative major

Return to E minor

Similar songs (chords in order of first appearance)

Chim-chim-cher-ee from *Mary Poppins* (chords Em, Em/D♯, Em/D, A/C♯, Am/C, Em/B F♯⁽⁷⁾/A♯, B⁽⁷⁾)

Edelweiss from *The sound of music* has a chromatic descending bass line in the last few bars (in C major, chords C, G⁽⁷⁾, F, Am, Dm, G, D⁽⁷⁾, C, Gm/B♭, F/A, Fm/A♭, C/G)

- Work out the chords for *Greensleeves* while you sing or hum the tune.
- Notice that the chorus begins on F, or chord ♭III, the relative major.
- Then work out the tune, remembering that both the 6th and 7th notes of the minor scale, B♭ and C, can be raised to become B and C♯. Try it hands together.

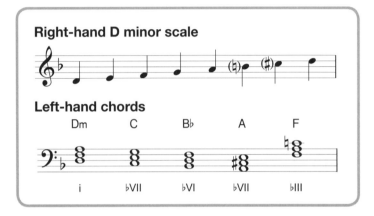

Similar songs (chords in order
of first appearance)

The animals went in two by two (chords Dm,
    F/C, F, C, B♭, A⁽⁷⁾)

The Snowman (chords Dm, C, Gm, B♭)

Pirates of the Caribbean (chords Dm, B♭, Am,
    F, C, Gm, A⁽⁷⁾)

Greensleeves

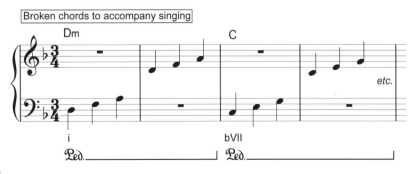

Improvising your own sixteen bars

Just as phrases are given letter names, so sections of music are given letter names so that the overall structure (or form) can be seen and understood. The most common is **binary form** which consists of two sections, A and B.

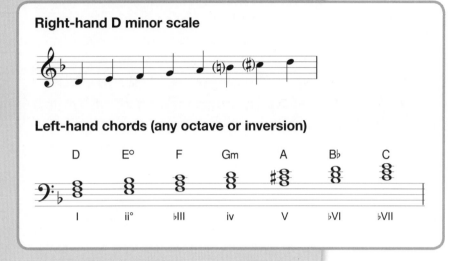

Right-hand D minor scale

Left-hand chords (any octave or inversion)

D	E°	F	Gm	A	B♭	C
I	ii°	♭III	iv	V	♭VI	♭VII

- Create your own improvisation in binary form. Section A begins in D minor, and B begins in F major and ends in D minor, as outlined.
- Choose your time signature and map out the chords using one chord per bar.
- When satisfied, play your whole progression with broken chords in both hands. Then play the chords in your left hand and improvise with your right hand.

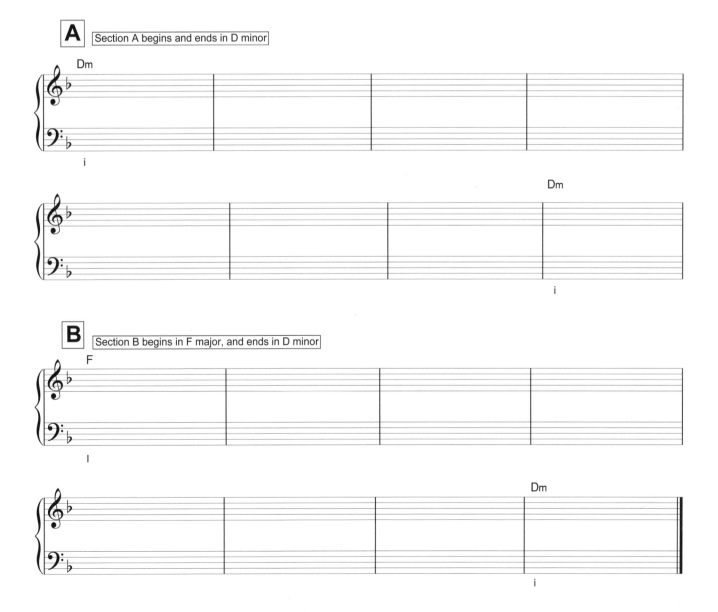

A Section A begins and ends in D minor

Dm

i

Dm

i

B Section B begins in F major, and ends in D minor

F

I

Dm

i

Transposition

Now that you know the primary chords in several keys, you can transpose them into other keys. The secret is to use the same fingering where possible, even when playing black notes.

Finding D major (or any other key)

- Play the left-hand primary chords in their usual inversions in D major (or your chosen new key), using finger memory and your ears to guide you.
- Play the right-hand scale by ear, noticing any sharps or flats.
- When secure, play the scale and chords together in the rhythm below (see page 26 for an example in C major).
- Finally, work out and name every chord in the key, in root position, and write them in.

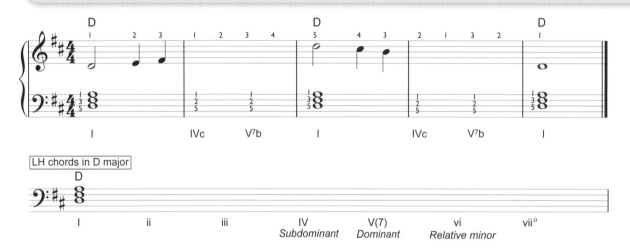

Ashokan farewell provides perfect practice for transposition because every chord in the key is needed.

- First, play it using the chords indicated (blocked or broken) in D major.
- When secure and comfortable, try transposing it to become more familiar with any other major key.

Ashokan farewell

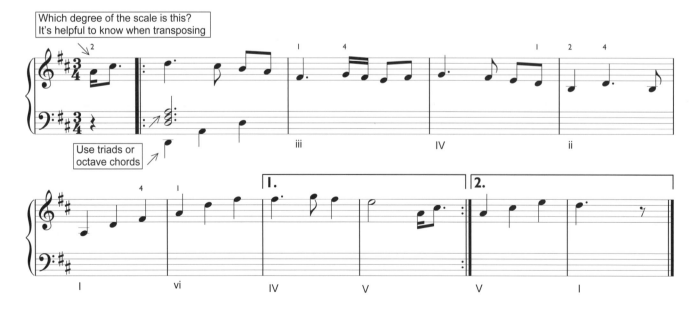

Similar songs (chords in order of first appearance)

It's not unusual Tom Jones (first section, chords D, Em⁽⁷⁾, F♯m, A⁽⁷⁾)
Be still in the presence of the Lord (chords D, F♯m⁷, Bm, Em⁷, A; chorus with chord G)
You raise me up Westlife (chords D, G, A, Bm)

The Arabian scale

Music for film and TV conveys atmosphere and emotion, telling us how to feel about the unfolding events. It can also tell us *where* the action is happening. This scale, with its two augmented seconds (E♭ to F♯ and B♭ to C♯) tells us immediately that we are somewhere in Arabia! Notice also the unusual chords: ♭II (E♭, G, B♭) and V♭5 (A, C♯, E♭). Chord VI+ (B♭, D, F♯) is an augmented chord, having a major third and augmented fifth.

- Piece together the ideas below with any of your own, to create music for an Arabian adventure.
- Your ideas can be general, or you can create a story set in a particular place (market or desert) with characters and events.

Right-hand Arabian scale

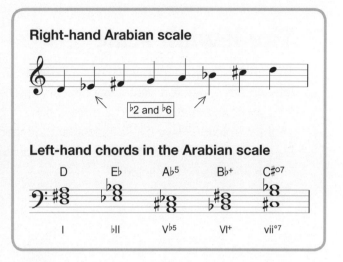

♭2 and ♭6

Left-hand chords in the Arabian scale

D	E♭	A♭5	B♭+	C♯°7
I	♭II	V♭5	VI+	vii°7

Tip

The more your story relates to your own experiences the more meaningful it will feel.

An Arabian adventure

Attention! (Setting the scene)

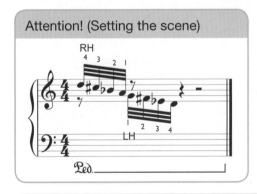

Happiness, contentment (right-hand improvises)

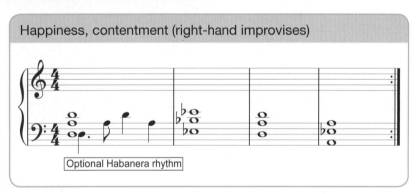

Optional Habanera rhythm

Wistfulness, longing (right-hand improvises)

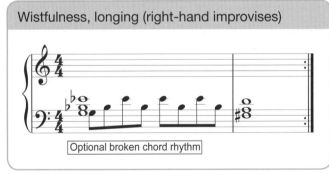

Optional broken chord rhythm

Peace, hope

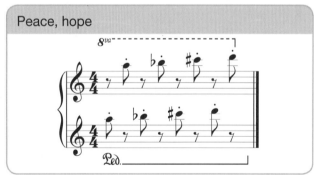

Wisdom, comfort (right-hand improvises)

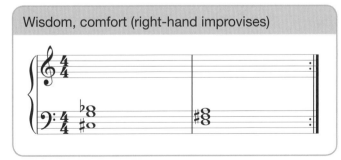

Fear, apprehension

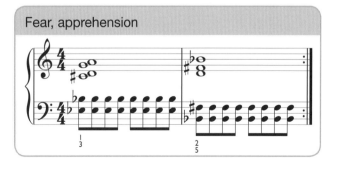

Song in the Arabian scale

Misirlou Nicolas Roubanis (only needs an open 5th chord on D)

The Jewish scale

The **Jewish** (or **Klezmer**) scale has a flattened 2nd, 6th and 7th compared to the major. It can also be thought of as a harmonic minor scale which begins on the dominant. *Hava nagila* is sung and danced at Barmitzvahs and weddings and is perhaps the best-known song using this scale.

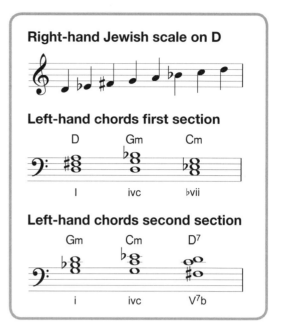

Right-hand Jewish scale on D

Left-hand chords first section

Left-hand chords second section

Hava nagila

Chord ♭II

The chord based on the flattened 2nd, chord ♭II, is characteristic of Jewish music and filled with yearning. Notice, too, that the chord on the flattened 7th, chord ♭vii, is minor in this key.

Jewish music is often accompanied by dance, usually the Hora, a circle dance originating in the Balkans, which typically has a six-beat dance step: walk-walk-step-kick-step-kick.

- Practise the Jewish scale and chords, and the two six-beat opening phrases. Then play them, and continue improvising.

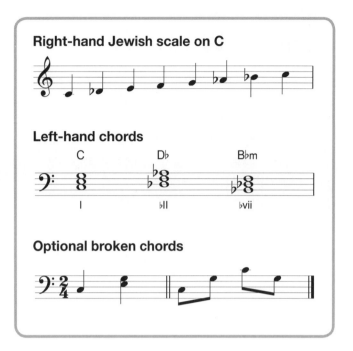

Right-hand Jewish scale on C

Left-hand chords

Optional broken chords

Improvise with the Jewish scale on C

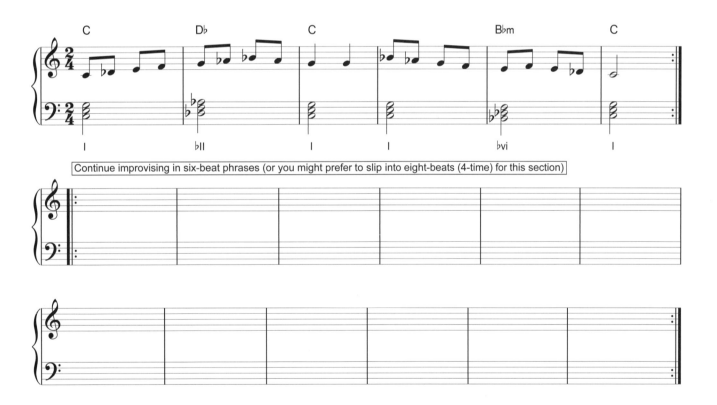

Continue improvising in six-beat phrases (or you might prefer to slip into eight-beats (4-time) for this section)

Similar songs (chords in order of first appearance)

Fiddler on the roof and *Tradition* (in C major, chords C, D♭)

Fly me to the moon (in C major, with circle of fifth chords Am, Dm⁷, G, C△, F, B°⁷, E, Am, then Dm, G⁷, C, Em, A⁷, Dm, D♭, C)

Tip

When the six-beat hora step is danced to Hava Nagila, it cuts across the eight-beat phrasing of the song, and feels exciting and energising!

111

Chord ♭VI

Chord ♭VI, based on the flattened 6th of the major scale, is often used as the third-to-last chord in a perfect cadence, giving the music a deeply felt and clearly defined end.

- Practise the left-hand chords, noticing that chord I (G) is used in second inversion, and chord ♭VI in this key is E♭ (E♭, G, B♭).
- Then sing or hum the tune while you work out the chords, and put hands together.
- Continue seamlessly into an improvisation.

Right-hand G major from the dominant (♭3)

Left-hand chords

G/D   D   E♭

Ic   V   ♭VI

Optional rhythm

G/D   D

I   V

Mister Cellophane from *Chicago*

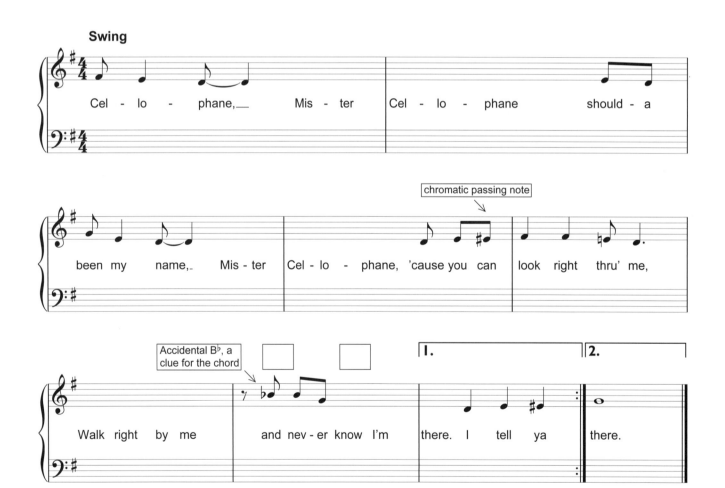

Swing

Cel - lo - phane,__ Mis - ter | Cel - lo - phane should - a

been my name,_ Mis - ter | Cel - lo - phane, 'cause you can | look right thru' me,

chromatic passing note

Walk right by me | and nev - er know I'm | *1.* there. I tell ya | *2.* there.

Accidental B♭, a clue for the chord

Similar songs (chords in order of first appearance)

Can't help Lovin' Dat Man from *Showboat* (in C, chorus chords C, Am, F, G⁷, A♭)

What a wonderful world Louis Armstrong (in F, chords F, Am, B♭, Gm, A⁷, Dm, D♭, C⁷)

Chord ♭III

Chord ♭III, on the flattened 3rd note of the scale, is used at the end of this song, conveying a sense of determination.

- Work out the chords while you sing or hum the tune. Notice that many chords anticipate the beat.
- Then play the right-hand tune with the left-hand chords.

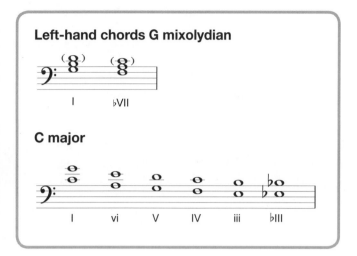

Let it go from *Frozen*

Similar songs (chords in order of first appearance)

Merry Xmas everybody Slade (chorus in C major, chords C, Em⁷, E♭, G)

Improvising with the blues

You are familiar with the flattened 3rd and flattened 7th notes of the scale. The flattened 5th (or raised 4th) is the other important note in creating the 'blues' sound:

- Practise the right-hand blues scale and left-hand twelve-bar blues.
- Then put together with a right-hand blues scale improvisation.
- Have fun improvising with any of the scales over the twelve-bar blues progression.

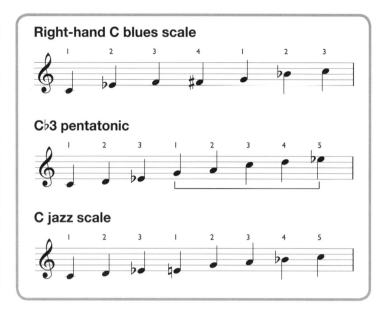

Right-hand C blues scale

C♭3 pentatonic

C jazz scale

Twelve bar blues in C

Songs based on twelve-bar blues

Johnny B. Goode Chuck Berry (the last line's chords are G, G, C, C)
Shake, rattle and roll (begins on C, the last line's chords are Dm⁷, G⁷, C, C)
Can't buy me love The Beatles (twelve-bar section last line's chords are G, F, F, C)

114

Blues songs tend to have few chords, and these are often just outlined in single-note bass lines. Melodies are usually based on the blues scale, but may also include other notes.

- Play the A minor pentatonic and then the A blues scale, noticing that the blues scale has just one additional note, D♯.
- When confident with the scale, practise the two-chord left hand below, and then improvise over it.

Notice that the progression ends on chord V. It needs to fade away to end.

Right-hand A minor pentatonic

A blues scale

the 'blue' note

Alternative left-hand basses

Improvise with the A blues scale

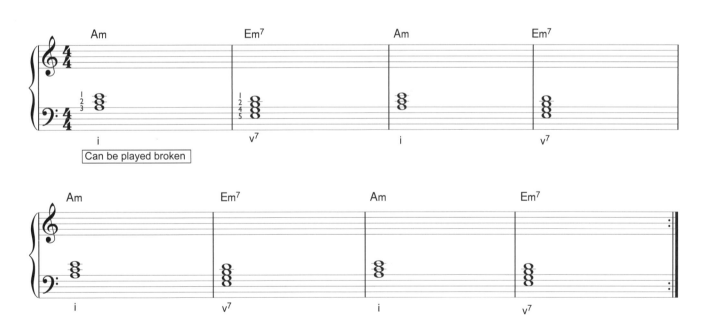

Can be played broken

Blues-style songs (chords in order of first appearance)

I need a dollar Aloe Blacc (chords Am, G, Dm)

Fever Peggy Lee (chords Am, E^7, F)

Catfish blues Jimi Hendrix (chords A^7 and Am^7 with A and E as a bass line)

Hit the road, Jack Ray Charles (chords Am, Am/G, F, E^7)

Fallin' Alisha Keys (in E minor, chords Em and Bm^7)

A ternary-form improvisation

Ternary form has three sections: A B A. Very often the first A is repeated (A A B A). Each section is usually eight bars in length, so the whole piece or song will be 24 or 32 bars altogether. In jazz and blues music, A is known as the **head**, and B as the **middle eight**.

- Practise the three left-hand basses and improvise over them with their corresponding blues scales.

- Then play an A minor bass improvisation (A), followed by one in either E or D minor (B) then repeat A again to create a ternary form improvisation (A B A).

- Finally, use the space below to compose two of your own repeated-bass patterns in any of the three minor keys. When satisfied, improvise over them with their corresponding blues scales. Notice the *da capo al fine*, so your improvisation will be in ternary form, A B A.

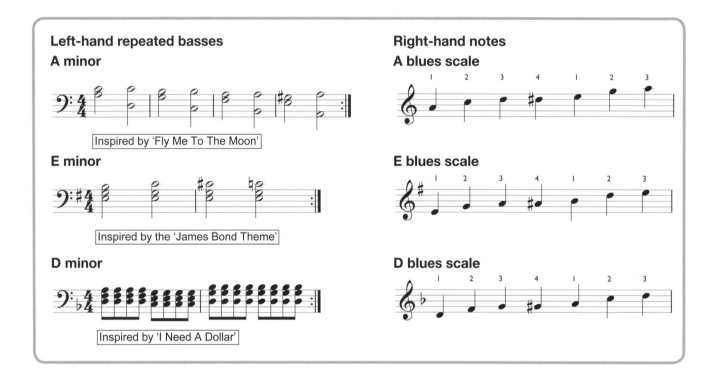

Left-hand repeated basses
A minor

Inspired by 'Fly Me To The Moon'

E minor

Inspired by the 'James Bond Theme'

D minor

Inspired by 'I Need A Dollar'

Right-hand notes
A blues scale

E blues scale

D blues scale

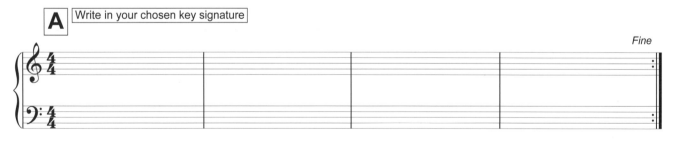

A | Write in your chosen key signature

Fine

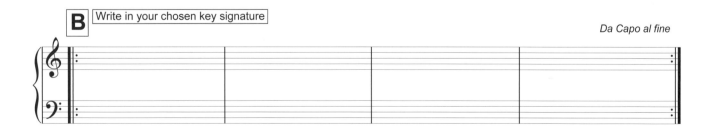

B | Write in your chosen key signature

Da Capo al fine

Solo or group improvising on the black-note twelve-bar blues

It's worth learning the twelve-bar blues in E♭ because the right-hand improvisation can be played solely on the black notes. Anyone, of any age and ability can join in.

You could also choose to improvise using the E♭ blues scale which is the black note minor pentatonic (the black notes from E♭), with the 'blue' note, A♮, slipped in.

Tip *If playing with two or more people, listen, copy and respond to each other's rhythms and ideas, so there is a sense of 'conversation' between everyone.*

Right-hand black notes
Any black notes can be played one at a time or in clusters (two or more notes at once) with any fingering. The key note is E♭.

E♭ blues scale

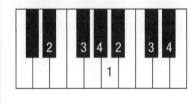

'blue note'

Four bar introduction

Twelve bars begin here

Improvising with your current piece

Let's pretend that your current piece is Burgmüller's *Arabesque* (opposite) and you want to be able to improvise around it. Not only will this help you understand and appreciate the music better and memorise it, but you will also be able to continue playing at length in the style of the piece, whether or not you can remember the original! As always, the key points are to:

- Keep the improvisation well within your technical ability
- Concentrate on maintaining a consistent pulse
- *Feel* more than *think*: follow your musical instinct
- Remember the chords
- Bring it to a musically satisfying end.

Here are four suggestions:

1 Identify the key (A minor) and look for the primary or other regularly used chords. Play grand arpeggios or broken-chord progressions with them.

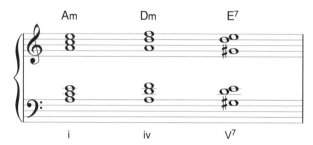

2 Identify two chords which can be played alternately in the left hand while the right improvises in a five-finger position.

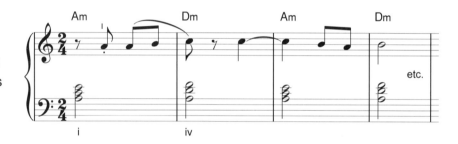

3 Use the opening 4-bar chord progression as a repeated bass. Begin with a 4-bar or 8-bar left-hand introduction, then improvise using a five-finger position or full scale.

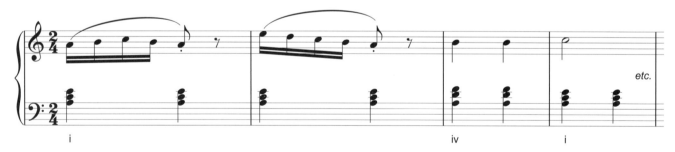

4 Choose your favourite chord progression (this is from bars 12-19). Reduce it to block chords, add a repeat and cadence. Then either play it with both hands as broken chords or left-hand chords with a right-hand improvised melody.

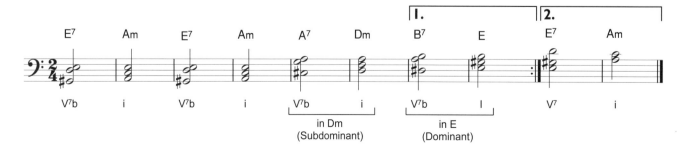

Arabesque

Friedrich Burgmüller

Playing more tunes by ear

Now that you have completed the book, here are some additional tips to help you play other tunes by ear.

1 **Decide on your key, and practise the chords in that key.** Choose a key you are familiar with, you can always transpose later. Run through the primary chords in their usual inversions (I, IVc and V⁷b). Then play all the chords of the key in root position, noticing particularly the dominant, subdominant and relative major/minor. You can also play the dominants of those chords (secondary dominants). Unless you are prepared for them, these chords are often the sticking points! Remember that you could also come across flattened chords, especially the chord on the flattened 7th, and other less-used chords which require careful listening. When the right chord proves elusive, just aim to find a single bass note that suggests the right chord.

2 **Work out the chord progression.** Once you have played through the chords in the key, you should be able to 'hear' the starting note and sing or hum the tune while you work out the chords. (If you can't 'hear' the starting note it may be because you practised chords in a major rather than minor key or vice versa.) You might want to write out the lyrics (you can usually download them), underline the strong syllables and jot down the relevant chord symbols as you become sure of them.

3 **When you know your chords, work out the tune.** Play the scale in your chosen key then work out the tune. Humming can help you identify whether the next note is higher or lower than the last, through the sensation inside your throat. It also helps to think whether the melody note harmonises with the left-hand chord, and so is a note of the chord, or whether it's a passing note or clashing note. Organise your fingering, phrase by phrase, into sensible and comfortable patterns to help you feel and remember what you're playing.

4 **Decide on your style of accompaniment, and put hands together.** You can play single bass notes, open 5ths or block or broken chords in your left hand, and single melody notes, double thirds or chords in your right hand. Remember you can choose to play the chords in both hands, in any suitable rhythm as an accompaniment. Try also playing the left-hand chords while improvising with your right hand.

Have fun! The more you do, the easier it becomes.

Ideas for improvisation at a glance

Scales

- Black-note pentatonics: major or minor
- White-note pentatonics: major, minor or ♭3
- White-note modes: Aeolian, Dorian, Phrygian, Lydian or Mixolydian
- Major or minor
- Jazz, Jewish, Arabian or blues

Frameworks and chord progressions

- Alternating single-note tonic (I) and dominant (V)
- Alternating open 5ths, 6ths and 7ths
- Two alternating chords, e.g. I, IV
- Repeating chord patterns, e.g. I, vi, IV, V
- Twelve-bar blues
- Circle of fifths
- Sequences and modulations
- Chord progressions from songs
- Your own eight, sixteen or twenty-four bar progression
- Binary (AB) or ternary (ABA) form

Left-hand accompaniments

- Open 5ths
- Full chords
- Broken chords in a variety of styles
- Single-line bass notes (or octaves)
- Descending and ascending bass lines
- Walking bass

Right-hand melodies

- Using the rhythm of a well-known song
- Thinking in phrase patterns, e.g. question and answer or A B A C
- Step-wise scale patterns
- Inversions and decorations
- Higher and lower octaves
- Double thirds
- Chords, including broken-chord melodies with passing notes

Sources of inspiration

- Songs and pieces of music
- Words: titles, themes, poems and stories
- Pictures and photos: nature, places, people and events
- Thoughts and feelings
- Movement and dance: a march, lullaby, waltz or knees up

Here are some ways to start improvising with your students. Try to include playing by ear or an improvising exercise every lesson, relating it in some way (key, chords, rhythm or melody) to the scales and pieces they are currently studying. You will be pleasantly surprised at their growing confidence.

Five-finger warm ups and improvisation

Teachers play an accompaniment while students first listen and then join in, playing up and down in time with the pulse. When confident, they can improvise. The accompaniments can be adapted for different keys and time signatures.

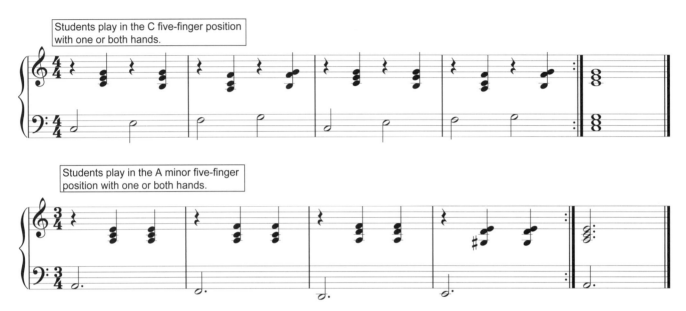

Three games: Examples are given on the black notes, but can be adapted to help students become familiar with any key or time signature.

1. Copy me: When confident, this can be reversed so students play for teachers to copy.

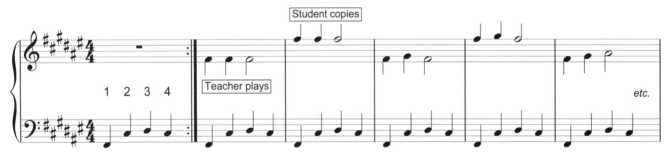

2. Question and answer: when confident this can be reversed.

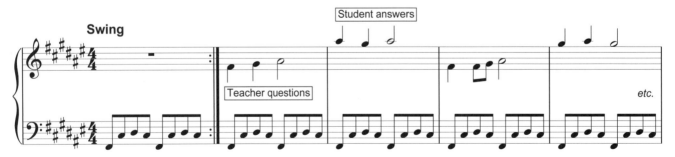

3. Free conversation: teachers and students improvise freely, listening and responding to each other. The black note twelve-bar blues, in which teachers play a left-hand chord progression and improvise in 'free conversation' with students on the black notes, is an excellent way to begin. See page 117.

Notes and scales

Musical notes have seven letter names: A B C D E F G, one for each white note of the piano. The black notes are both sharps (one semitone higher than the white note of the same name) and flats (one semitone lower).

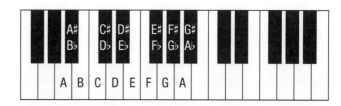

The distance from one note to another is known as an interval. The smallest interval from one note to the next (black or white) is a semitone (or half-step). The interval from one note to the next note of the same letter name is an octave (eight notes). There are twelve semitones in an octave.

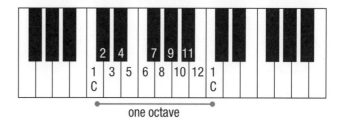

one octave

A tone (or whole-step) is the interval of two semitones. There are six tones in an octave.

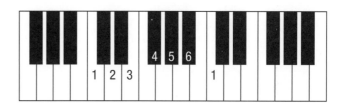

The distinctive sound of different scales is created by the different order of tones, semitones and other intervals within it. The order of tones and semitones within the eight notes of a major scale are:

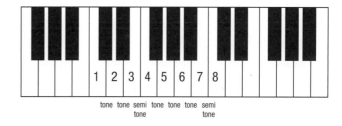

tone tone semi tone tone tone semi
tone   tone

The following scales appear in this book. They are described here from C, for easy comparison.

Major: C D E F G A B C
Minor: C D Eb F G Ab Bb C
Pentatonic major: C D E G A C
Flat 3 pentatonic: C D Eb G A C
Pentatonic minor: C Eb F G Bb C
Jazz scale: C D Eb E G A Bb C
Harmonic minor: C D Eb F G Ab B C
Dorian mode: C D Eb F G A Bb C
Phrygian mode: C Db Eb F G Ab Bb C
Lydian mode: C D E F# G A B C
Mixolydian mode: C D E F G A Bb C
Aeolian mode: C D Eb F G Ab Bb C
Arabian: C Db E F G Ab B C
Jewish (Klezmer):   C Db E F G Ab Bb C
Blues scale: C Eb F F# G Bb C

Intervals and chords

Intervals

A semitone (half-step) is also known as the interval of a **minor 2nd**, and a tone (whole-step) is a **major 2nd**.

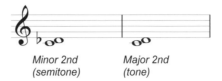

These are the intervals formed by the notes of a major scale:

These are the intervals formed by the notes of a natural minor scale:

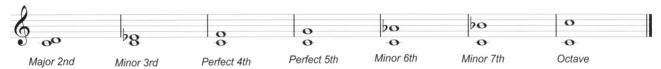

Augmented intervals are one semitone larger than major and perfect intervals. **Diminished** intervals are one semitone smaller than minor and perfect intervals. Here are some examples:

Chords and chord symbols

It is useful to be aware of the intervals used to create different types of chords. The following chords appear in this book (here shown from C for easy comparison).

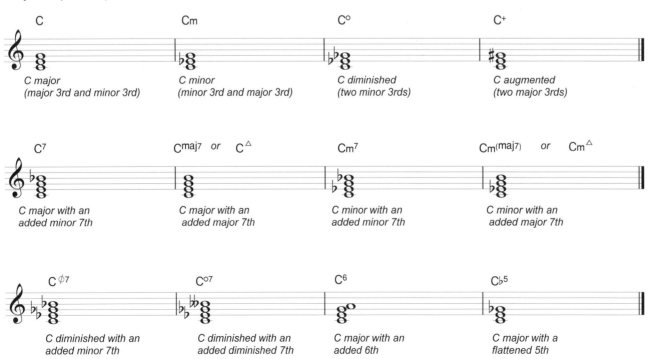

Glossary of terms

1950s chord progression Chord progression I vi IV V that became popular in the 1950s. *(page 80)*

Accompaniment Usually in the left hand, played below the melody. *(page 20)*

Aeolian mode The Aeolian mode is the natural minor: a minor scale without the raised 7th. *(page 77)*

Arabian scale A scale containing two augmented seconds. *(page 109)*

Bass line A bass line is created by the lowest notes of root position or inverted chords. *(page 90)*

Binary form A musical form which consists of two sections, A and B. *(page 107)*

Blues scale A six-note scale with a flattened 3rd, flattened 5th and flattened 7th. *(page 114)*

Broken chord Playing each note of a chord in turn, usually starting at the bottom. *(page 16)*

Cadence A two-chord progression found at the end of phrases, sections and pieces of music. *(page 23)*

Calypso From the Caribbean, featuring a distinctive quaver rhythm emphasising the first, fourth and seventh quavers of each bar. *(page 50)*

Chords The simultaneous sounding of two or more notes to produce harmony. Chords are named by the root note. *(page 16)*

Chromatic passing notes Notes that are not included in either the scale or the current chord. *(page 94)*

Circle of fifths A sequence of chords which move down by a 5th each time. *(page 102)*

Clashing notes Notes which clash with the accompaniment; they often resolve onto a harmony note on the following beat. *(page 24)*

Da capo al fine Repeat from the beginning and go to the word 'fine'. *(page 116)*

Diatonic passing notes Notes from the scale that are not part of the accompanying chord. *(page 94)*

Diminished chord A chord with a minor third and a flattened or 'diminished' fifth. *(page 79)*

Dominant The fifth degree of the scale and the chord built on that note. *(page 17)*

Dominant seventh Chord V (the dominant) with an added minor 7th. *(page 21)*

Doo-wop progression Chords I vi ii V. Developed from the 1950s chord progression, substituting chord ii for chord IV. *(page 81)*

Dorian mode A modal scale with flattened 3rd and 7th notes compared to the major scale. *(page 74)*

Downbeat or strong beat The first beat of the bar. *(page 8)*

Fine The end or finish. *(page 116)*

First inversion A chord with the 3rd (middle note) as the bass note. *(page 17)*

Form The overall structure of a piece of music. *(page 6)*

Grand arpeggio Broken chords spread between the hands played all the way up the keyboard. *(page 16)*

Harmony Chords and their progressions. *(page 6)*

Harmonic rhythm The rate at which chords change. *(page 85)*

Harmony notes Notes which are part of a chord. *(page 24)*

Head The main theme of a piece of music. *(page 116)*

Imperfect cadence The chord progression chord I (or any chord) to chord V. *(page 23)*

Improvisation Spontaneous performance in which the music is made up. *(page 12)*

Inversions of chords Chords with notes other than the root in the bass. *(page 17)*

Ionian mode A mode which uses the same pattern of notes as the major scale. *(page 72)*

Jazz scale Created from a combination of the major scale and the pentatonic with a ♭3 and ♭7. *(page 81)*

Jewish scale The Jewish (or Klezmer) scale has a flattened 2nd, 6th and 7th compared to the major scale. *(page 110)*

Key or tonality The scale or group of notes a piece is based on, and their 'home' base. *(page 6)*

Key chord (or home chord) The chord on the first degree of the scale. *(page 18)*

Key-note (or 'home note') The first degree of the scale, also known as the tonic. *(page 8)*

Key signature A group of accidentals at the start of a piece indicating the key. *(page 38)*

Lead sheets Music notation that gives the melody, lyrics and chord symbols only. *(page 19)*

Leading note The seventh degree of the scale. *(page 79)*

Mediant The third degree of a scale and the chord built on that note. *(page 79)*

Melody The tune. *(page 6)*

Middle eight A contrasting section in a song (not necessarily eight bars). *(page 116)*

Minor chord A chord built up of a root, minor 3rd and perfect 5th. *(page 65)*

Mixolydian mode A mode with a flattened 7th note compared to the major scale. *(page 76)*

Modes Seven-note scales which can be found by playing an octave of 'white notes' on the piano, each with a different starting note. *(page 72)*

Modulation Changing key within a piece. *(page 40)*

Octaves The distance between two notes with the same letter name. *(page 29)*

Passing notes Notes which pass between chord notes. *(page 24)*

Perfect cadence The chord progression chord V to chord I. *(page 23)*

Pentatonic From the Greek word 'pente', meaning five. Pentatonic scales have five notes. *(page 6)*

Phrases Short sections of music that combine to form an entire song or piece. *(page 30)*

Pitch The rise and fall of notes in relation to each other. *(page 6)*

Plagal cadence The progression chord IV to chord I. *(page 67)*

Primary chords Chords I, IV and V (and V⁷) are the primary chords in any key. *(page 26)*

Pub-style accompaniments Characterised by a 'boom ching' rhythm between left and right hands. *(page 91)*

Pulse The underlying beat of a piece of music. *(page 6)*

Relative minor All major keys have a relative minor that shares the same key signature. *(page 65)*

Repeated bass A bass note or pattern played repeatedly. *(page 15)*

Rhythm The length of notes and how they are grouped together in patterns over time. *(page 6)*

Roman numerals Roman numerals indicate which degree of the scale a chord is built. *(page 16)*

Root or tonic The first degree of a scale and the chord built on that note. *(page 16)*

Root position A chord arranged with the root as the lowest note. *(page 17)*

Scale A pattern of notes arranged in order from low to high. *(page 6)*

Secondary chords These are chords ii (supertonic), iii (mediant) and vi (submediant). *(page 79)*

Secondary dominants Dominant sevenths built on chords other than the dominant. *(page 93)*

Secondary dominant sequences A classic chord progression that rises through tonic – dominant sequences. *(page 96)*

Second inversion A chord with the fifth note as the bass note. *(page 17)*

Strong beat *see* **Downbeat**

Subdominant The fourth degree of a scale and the chord built on that note. *(page 25)*

Submediant The sixth degree of a scale and the chord built on that note. *(page 79)*

Supertonic The second degree of a scale and the chord built on that note. *(page 79)*

Swing Quaver notes are played ♩ ♪. *(page 79)*

Syncopation The effect created when off-beat notes are accented. *(page 43)*

Ternary form A musical work in three sections: A B A. In jazz and blues music, A is known as the head, and B as the middle eight. *(page 116)*

Tierce de Picardie The use of a major tonic chord at the end of a minor or modal musical section. *(page 71)*

Tonic *see* **Root**

Transposition Changing the key of a piece to another key. *(page 39)*

Triads A triad consists of the first (also known as the root), third and fifth notes of a scale. *(page 16)*

Twelve-bar blues A common 12-bar chord progression in jazz and blues. *(page 43)*

Upbeat (or **anacrusis**) A phrase that begins on something other than the first beat of the bar. *(page 9)*

Walking bass A chord progression outlined in single notes, often played by the double bass or the left hand on a piano. *(page 62)*

Ashoken Farewell
Music by Jay Ungar
© 1983 Swinging Door Music
Warner/Chappell North America Ltd
All Rights Reserved.

Heart and Soul
Words by Frank Loesser
© 1939 Sony/ATV Harmony
Sony/ATV Harmony UK
All Rights Reserved.

I'd Do Anything (from *Oliver*)
Words and Music by Lionel Bart
© 1960 Lakeview Music Publishing Co Ltd
All Rights Reserved.

Let It Go (from *Frozen*)
Words and Music by Robert Lopez and Kristen Anderson-Lopez
© 2013 Wonderland Music Company Inc administered by Artemis Muziekuitgeverij B.V.
Warner/Chappell Artemis Music Ltd
All Rights Reserved.

Let's Twist Again
Words and Music by Kal Mann and David Appell
© 1961 (renewed) Kalmann Music Inc
All Rights for the world outside the United States administered by Chappell & Co
All Rights Reserved
Reproduced by kind permission of Carlin Music Corp., London NW1 8BD

Merrily We Roll Along
Words by Murray Mencher
Music by Charles Tobias and Eddie Cantor
© 1935 (Renewed) WB Music Corp
Warner/Chappell North America Ltd
All Rights Reserved.

Mister Cellophane
Words by Fred Ebb
Music by John Kander
© 1975 Kander & Ebb Inc and Unichappell Music Inc
Warner/Chappell North America Ltd
All Rights Reserved.

Nine To Five
Words and Music by Dolly Parton
© 1980 Velvet Apple Music
All Rights Reserved
Reproduced by kind permission of Carlin Music Corporation, London, NW1 8BD

The Power of Love
Words and Music by Mark O'Toole, Brian Nash, Holly Johnson and Peter Gill
© 1984 Perfect Songs Ltd
All Rights Reserved.

Step In Time (from *Mary Poppins*)
Words and Music by Richard M. Sherman and Robert B. Sherman
© 1964 Wonderland Music Company Inc administered by Artemis Muziekuitgeverij B.V.
Warner/Chappell Artemis Music Ltd
All Rights Reserved.

Stranger In Paradise
Words and Music by George Chet Forrest and Bob Wright
© 1955 Scheffel Music Corp
Warner/Chappell Music Ltd
All Rights Reserved.

Will You Go, Lassie, Go (aka **Wild Mountain Thyme**)
Words and Music by The McPeake Family Trio
© 1962 English Folk Dance And Song Society
Chappell Music Ltd
All Rights Reserved.

Lyrics only:
Bad Moon Rising
Words by John Fogerty
© 1964 Jondora Music
Burlington Music Co Ltd
All Rights Reserved.

Merrily We Roll Along
Words by Murray Mencher
© 1935 (Renewed) WB Music Corp
Warner/Chappell North America Ltd
All Rights Reserved.

Index of song titles